1 MONTH OF
FREE
READING

at

www.ForgottenBooks.com

By purchasing this book you are
eligible for one month membership to
ForgottenBooks.com, giving you
unlimited access to our entire
collection of over 700,000 titles via
our web site and mobile apps.

To claim your free month visit:

www.forgottenbooks.com/free49760

ISBN 978-0-267-49190-2
PIBN 10049760

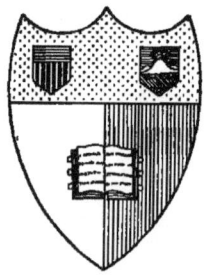

THE

WISCONSIN INCOME TAX LAW

WITH EXPLANATORY NOTES

FOURTH EDITION

WISCONSIN TAX COMMISSION

MADISON, WIS.

1919

THE

WISCONSIN INCOME TAX LAW

WITH EXPLANATORY NOTES

FOURTH EDITION

ISSUED BY

WISCONSIN TAX COMMISSION
MADISON, WIS.

1919

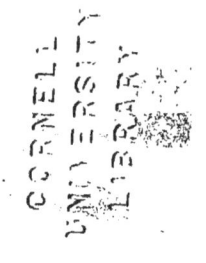

MADISON, WISCONSIN
DEMOCRAT PRINTING COMPANY, STATE PRINTER

A496000

PREFACE

The fundamental principle of the income tax law is to tax annually net incomes within the jurisdiction of this state. This basic principle should not be lost sight of either by taxpayers or tax officials when dealing with income taxation. Net income is what remains of gross income after deducting the expenses of producing it and certain other charges specifically allowed as deductions by statute. No deductions from gross income are allowable except such as are authorized by law.

Every individual receiving taxable income is required to report annually to the assessor of incomes in his district on forms prepared by the tax commission the amounts of income received by him during the previous year from all sources. All corporations doing business in this state must make like reports to the tax commission. Corporations and individuals should also report on the same blank used in reporting income all necessary expenses incurred in producing the same and all statutory deductions.

If it were perfectly clear in all cases just what under the law is income and just what is legally deductible and all taxpayers religiously complied with the law in making returns, the task of the tax commission and of income tax assessors would be simple. But failure on the part of taxpayers to understand fully just where the line runs between receipts that are income and those that are not and to distinguish between expenditures that are deductible and those that are not, opens up an extensive field for investigation on the part of tax officials.

This pamphlet contains the Wisconsin income tax law of 1911, as amended in 1913, 1915, 1917, and 1919, together with citations to decisions of the supreme court, and to some of the important rulings of the tax commission under appropriate sections. It is published as an aid to assessors of incomes and taxpayers in performing the important duties imposed upon them. Familiarity with the law and conscientious observance of it on the part of taxpayers will simplify the preparation of income tax returns, limit the scope of inquiry on the part of tax officials, and in every way promote efficient and satisfactory administration.

Taxpayers are invited to seek the advice and counsel of the tax commission and assessors of incomes, either in person or by letter when in doubt as to what the law requires of them.

WISCONSIN TAX COMMISSION.

THE WISCONSIN INCOME TAX LAW

Chapter 658, Laws of 1911; sections 1087m—1 to 1087m—30
of the statutes.

PART I

For what period tax levied

SECTION 1087m—1. There shall be assessed, levied, collected
and paid a tax upon incomes received during the year ending
December 31, 1911, and upon incomes received annually thereafter, by such persons and from such sources as hereinafter de-
scribed; provided, that firms, copartnerships, corporations, joint
stock companies and associations which customarily close their
annual accounts on a date other than December 31, or which
customarily estimate their income or profits on a basis other than
of actual cash receipts and disbursements, may, with the consent
and approval of the tax commission, return for assessment and
taxation the income or profits earned during the business year
for which the accounts of such person are customarily made up.

In general, all persons must make their returns for the income received during the calendar year; but firms, copartnerships, corporations, etc., *may*, by securing the consent of the tax
commission, base their returns upon their respective fiscal years.

Definition of "person"

SECTION 1087m—2. 1. The term "person," as used in this
act, shall mean and include any individual, firm, copartnership,
and every corporation, joint stock company or association organized for profit, and having a capital stock represented by
shares, unless otherwise expressly stated.

In the following pages the word "individuals" is used where
natural persons are referred to and the word "corporations"
as the equivalent of "corporation, joint stock company or association organized for profit."

What income includes

SECTION 1087m—2. 2. The term "income," as used in this act, shall include:

(a) All rent of real estate. *(1917 c. 374.)*

(b) All dividends derived from stocks and all interest derived from money loaned or invested in notes, mortgages, bonds or other evidence of debt of any kind whatsoever, provided, that the term "dividends" as used in this section shall be held to mean any distribution made by a corporation, joint stock company or association, out of its earnings or profits accrued since January 1, 1911, and paid to its shareholders whether in cash or in stock of the corporation, joint company or association. *(1917 c. 247.)*

(c) All wages, salaries or fees derived from services; provided, that compensation to public officers for public service shall not be computed as a part of the taxable income in such cases where the taxation thereof would be repugnant to the constitution.

(d) All profits derived from the transaction of business or from the sale of real estate or other capital assets; provided, that for the purpose of ascertaining the gain or loss resulting from the sale or other disposition of property, real or personal, acquired prior to January 1, 1911, the fair market value of such property as of January 1, 1911, shall be the basis for determining the amount of such gain or loss. *(1917 c 248.)*

(e) All royalties derived from mines or the possession or use of franchises or legalized privileges of any kind.

(f) And all other gains, profits or income of any kind derived from any source whatever except such as hereinafter exempted. *(1913 c. 720.)*

It will be observed that the meaning of the term "income" as defined in the income tax law of 1911 was modified by the amendments of 1917 in the following respects:

1st. "Estimated rental of residence property occupied by the owner" was eliminated.

2d. "Dividends" were limited to a distribution of corporate earnings accrued since January 1, 1911.

3d. The fair market value of capital assets acquired prior to January 1, 1911, and sold during any subsequent year was fixed as the basis from which to determine the profit or loss on the sale.

Whatever property or thing of value the taxpayer had at the time the income tax law took effect was capital and no part of such capital could be made into income by legislative enactment. *State ex rel. Bundy vs. Nygaard,* 163 Wis. 307.

The word "income" as used in the constitution means the profit or gain derived from capital or labor, or both combined. *State ex rel. Wisconsin Trust Co. vs. Widule*, 164 Wis. 56. It may be money or that which is convertible into money. *Income Tax Cases*, 148 Wis. 456.

Strictly speaking, income as contrasted with capital denotes that amount of wealth which flows in during a definite period and which is at the disposal of the owner for purposes of consumption so that in consuming it his capital remains unimpaired. Seligman on Income Tax, 19.

The amendment to sec. 1, art. **VIII** of the constitution authorizes the legislature to tax incomes in any case where the state has power to impose such a tax and hence includes the power to tax the salaries of all state and local officers, including the salaries of circuit judges elected before the income tax law was adopted. *State ex rel. Wickham v. Nygaard*, 159 Wis. 396. In the same case the court intimated that salaries of federal officers and compensation of employes of the federal government are not subject to taxation under state income tax laws and the attorney general has advised to the same effect. See also *Dobbins v. Erie County*, 16 Peters, 435, and *Purnell v. Page*, 133 N. C. 125. Neither the state nor federal government has power to tax the agencies or instrumentalities employed by the other in carrying on its governmental functions. It would seem to follow from this principle that interest on United States bonds or other securities issued by the federal government is not taxable under our income tax law and assessors of incomes are advised to omit such income in making their assessments.

Dividends declared and paid out of reserves for depreciation, bad accounts, etc., are income and should be assessed either to stockholders receiving them or to corporations paying them. The reason for this is that the reserves set aside from earnings have been overestimated and found to exceed the requirements which they were originally designed to meet. The amount of such excess is definitely determined by its distribution as dividends and represents a profit to be accounted for as income. Dividends of this character should not be omitted from income tax returns under the pretense that they are a distribution of capital assets. The U. S. Treasury Department has recently made substantially the same rule under the federal income tax law. T. D. 2540, Income Tax Service, page 433.

Income of residents and nonresidents

SECTION 1087m—2. 3. The tax shall be assessed, levied and collected upon all income, not hereinafter exempted, received by every person residing within the state, and by every nonresident of the state, upon such income as is derived from property located or business transacted within the state. In determining taxable income, rentals, royalties, and gains or profit from the operation of any farm, mine, or quarry shall follow the situs of the property from which derived, and income from personal service and from land contracts, mortgages, stocks, bonds and securities shall follow the residence of the recipient. With respect to other income, persons engaged in business within and without the state shall be taxed only upon such income as is derived from business transacted and property located within the state, which may be determined by an allocation and separate accounting for such income when made in form and manner prescribed by the tax commission, but otherwise shall be determined in the manner specified in subdivision (e) of subsection 7 of section 1770b of the statutes, as far as applicable. *(1913 c. 720.)*

A resident of this state is taxable on all his income derived from property located and business transacted within the state and also on all income from personal services, land contracts, mortgages, stocks, bonds and securities.

A nonresident is taxable on all income derived from property located and business transacted within this state, but not on income derived from personal services, land contracts, mortgages, stocks, bonds and securities.

An "allocation or separate accounting" is permissible where such an accounting would reflect correctly the income fairly attributable to Wisconsin. Corporations seldom keep their records by states and a correct separate accounting is ordinarily impossible. Consequently the apportionment method prescribed by subdivision (e) of subsection 7 of 1770b must usually be resorted to. This subdivision is as follows:

"In determining the proportion of capital stock employed in the state, the same shall be computed by taking the gross business in dollars of the corporation in the state and add[ing] the same to the full value in dollars of the property of the corporation located in the state. The sum so obtained shall be the numerator of a fraction of which the denominator shall consist of the total gross business in dollars of the corporation, both within and without the state, added to the full value in dollars of the entire property of the corporation, both within and without the state. The fraction so obtained shall represent the proportion of the capital stock represented within the state.''

In the case of manufacturing corporations the process of apportionment under the statute quoted is as follows: to get the numerator of the fraction take the full book value of the property owned in Wisconsin on December 31 of the income year, excluding land contracts, mortgages, stocks, bonds, and securities, farms, mines, quarries and property yielding rents or royalties, and to this amount add gross sales in Wisconsin; from the sum so obtained subtract the factory cost of goods sold in Wisconsin and add the factory cost of all products manufactured in Wisconsin. To get the denominator apply the same process to property and business everywhere.

The following example will illustrate the process:

1. Full book value of property in Wisconsin on December 31st, except as above stated	$50,000
Gross sales in Wisconsin during the year	100,000
	$150,000
2. Deduct factory cost of products sold in Wisconsin	50,000
	$100,000
3. Factory cost of products manufactured in Wisconsin..	200,000
Numerator	$300,000
4. Full book value of property everywhere except as above stated	$200,000
Gross sales everywhere	300,000
	$500,000
5. Deduct factory cost of products sold	200,000
	$300,000
6. Factory cost of products manufactured everywhere...	200,000
Denominator	$500,000

$$\frac{300,000}{500,000} = .60$$

Net income, $50,000 \times .60 = \$30,000$, taxable in Wisconsin. Tax, $1,640.00.

Where a corporation is engaged in buying or selling goods and merchandise within and without the state and does no manufacturing in the state, it should report the cost of purchases in the state instead of cost of products.

The rule of apportionment applies to individuals as well as corporations.

Income from rentals, royalites, gains or profits from the op·eration of any farm, mine, or quarry, is not apportionable for the reason. that such income has its *situs* for taxation purposes at the place where the property from which it is derived is located. Income from personal services, land contracts, mortgages, stocks, bonds, and securities is not apportionable for the reason that such income has its *situs* at the residence of the recipient. Nonapportionable income and the property from which it is derived must therefore be disregarded in making an apportionment of income from sources within and without the state. If such income is assignable to Wisconsin because of its *situs* it should be added to the apportionable income assigned to Wisconsin; if not, it is not Wisconsin income, and therefore not taxable.

The income received by a resident of the state from a copartnership of which he is a member and which is doing business and has all its property located outside the state, all the profits distributed being derived from sources without the state, is not taxable under this statute. *State ex rel. Arpin v. Eberhardt,* 158 Wis. 20, 22.

The income of a domestic manufacturing corporation derived from the sale of its products, manufactured in this state, to customers in this and other states, whether delivered directly from the factory to such customers or shipped to branch houses in other states and thence delivered to customers residing outside of the state on sales made either by the home office or by the branch houses, is income "derived from business transacted and property located within this state," within the meaning of sub. 3, sec. 1087m—2, Stats. 1911. The fact that the business so conducted involves transactions in interstate commerce does not affect the *situs* of the income; nor does the imposition by the state of a tax upon such income contravene sec. 8, art. 1, Const. of U. S., conferring upon Congress the power to regulate commerce between the states. That part of the income of such a corporation which is derived from goods produced and purchased outside of the state and shipped, either directly or by way of the home office in this state, to branch houses in other states and hence sold and delivered to customers without the state, is not attributable to business transacted within the state and is not taxable under the statute. *United States Glue Co. v. Oak Creek,* 161 Wis. 211; 247 U. S. 321.

DEDUCTIONS ALLOWED CORPORATIONS

SECTION 1087m—3.   Every corporation, joint stock company or association shall be allowed to make from its gross income the following deductions:

Wages and salaries

(a) Payments made within the year for wages of employees and salaries of officers if reasonable in amount, for services actually rendered producing such income; provided, there be reported the name, address and amount paid each such employee or officer residing within this state to whom a compensation of seven hundred dollars or more shall have been paid during the assessment year. *(1913 c. 720.)*

Under this provision the tax commission is authorized to disallow or reduce salaries which in its judgment are excessive or when the services rendered did not contribute to the income reported. All corporations doing business in the state, whether liable for an income tax or not, are required to furnish a list of their employes and officers residing in Wisconsin who receive a compensation of more than seven hundred dollars a year, and the amount paid to each. Failure to furnish such information will defeat the deduction.

(b) Other ordinary and necessary expenses and cash bonuses to employees, actually paid within the year out of the income in the maintenance and operation of its business and property, including a reasonable allowance for depreciation by use, wear and tear of property from which the income is derived and in the case of mines and quarries an allowance for depletion of ores and other natural deposits on the basis of their actual original cost in cash or the equivalent of cash; and including also interest paid during the year in the operation of the business from which its income is derived; provided, the debtor reports the amount so paid, the form of the indebtedness, together with the names and addresses of the parties to whom interest was paid. *(1917 c. 231.)*

Payments made for additions or improvements are not "ordinary or necessary expenses" and are not deductible from income. "Repairs" properly defined are deductible, but renewals or replacements of entire units of property, such as machines, are properly covered by depreciation, past or current, do not constitute "repairs," and cannot be deducted from income.

Depreciation, if claimed as a deduction, should be entered on the corporation books, to prevent confusion and duplication in returns. Depreciation is limited to deterioration or exhaustion "by use, wear and tear," and does not cover fluctations in market value. Depreciation of merchants' stocks cannot be allowed as such since it is properly cared for in the inventories, if the goods are still on hand, or if they have been sold, is properly represented in the decreased receipts from sales. Moreover the inventories at the beginning and end of the year must be on the same basis; if at the beginning of the year stock is inventoried at cost, it must be so inventoried at the end of the year.

This section removes the limitations on the amount of interest deduction that could be allowed corporations contained in the original act. Such deduction is, however, limited to that paid during the year in the operation of the business from which its (taxable) income is derived. Interest paid on borrowed money to carry on operations without the state, the income from which would not be taxable, and interest paid in holding and maintaining unproductive property cannot be allowed as a deduction. To be a proper deduction the interest paid must be related to and a factor in producing the income taxed.

Unless the corporation reports the form of the indebtedness, the amount paid, and the names and addresses of the parties who received it, no deduction for interest can be allowed. In order to secure this deduction care should be taken to comply with this section in making income returns.

By the foregoing subdivision depreciation is limited, 1st, to that occurring during the year in which the income is earned; 2nd, to that of property from which the income is derived; 3rd, to that resulting from "use, wear and tear." Furthermore it must be reasonable in amount. Unless depreciation claimed falls within these limitations it cannot be allowed as a deduction.

In arriving at the proper amount to be allowed for depreciation the factors to be considered are cost and estimated physical life of the property depreciated. The first factor can usually be determined without difficulty. The second can only be approximated. On page 56 of this pamphlet will be found tables of depreciation which experience has proved to be fairly correct. Taxpayers in making returns are requested to follow these tables.

Obsolescence is not a factor in determining depreciation in any case. There is absolutely no rule by which depreciation from obsolescence can be determined in advance and any attempt to do so is pure speculation. Besides depreciation from this cause is clearly excluded by the statute.

No depreciation of ''good will'' can be allowed as a deduction. The life of ''good will'' is indeterminate and in any case would be a mere guess. Neither does it deteriorate from ''use, wear and tear.'' In fact it not infrequently happens that the ''good will'' of a business is increasing in value while it is being charged off.

A stockholder cannot be permitted to deduct under the ''guise'' of losses depreciation in the value of his stock caused by the distribution of dividends. *Van Dyke vs. City of Milwaukee,* 159 Wis. 460.

In making a return for income taxation the lessee of a mine on a royalty basis is not entitled to make any deductions for ore depletion in addition to the sum paid as royalty. Even if the lease or right to mine is perpetual, it is not, for purposes of income taxation equivalent to ownership. *Klar Piquett Mining Co. vs. Platteville,* 163 Wis. 214, 215.

Royalties paid the fee owner by a lessee are deductible, whether paid at the date of entering into the lease or in annual payments, or both.

Cash bonuses voluntarily paid to employees over and above their regular wages may be deducted by the employer as expenses and in consequence should be reported as wages in making their individual return by employes.

Losses

(c) Losses actually sustained within the year and not compensated for by insurance or otherwise, provided that no loss resulting from the operation of business or the ownership of property may be allowed as a deduction, unless the income which might be derived from such business or property would be subject to taxation under this act. *(1919 c. 275.)*

The fact that a person purchased bonds at a premium does not entitle him to deduct annually from the interest received *pro rata* share of such premium in order that the capital may be kept unimpaired and that it may not be taxed as income. *Van Dyke vs. City of Milwaukee,* 159 Wis. 460.

Accounts and bills receivable charged off the books as worthless during the year may be allowed as deductions if previously reported as income.

The exact amount of the loss and the manner in which it occurred must be fully set forth in the return in order to secure the deduction.

Taxes

(d) Sums paid by such person within the year for taxes imposed upon the source from which the income taxed by this act is derived by any state of this union or subdivision thereof, or any territory or possession of the United States, or the United States government as income, excess profits or war profits taxes. *(1919 c. 435.)*

This section refers to general taxes paid upon property from which the income is derived. Taxes paid upon unimproved real estate and upon idle property held for investment or speculation cannot be deducted. Income taxes, excess profits and war taxes paid in cash may be deducted. Taxes paid by corporations cannot be allowed as deductions from the income of the stockholder. Special assessments cannot be considered as taxes because they are based on the theory that the property is benefited to the amount of the special assessment imposed.

Dividends

(e) Dividends or income received within the year from stocks or interest in any copartnership, corporation, joint stock company or association, the income of which shall have been assessed under the provisions of this act; provided that when only part of the income of the copartnership, corporation, joint stock company or association from which such dividend or income was received shall have been assessed under this act only a corresponding part of such dividend or income shall be deducted; provided, further, that such copartnership, corporation, joint stock company or association report the name and address of each person owning stocks or having such interest and the amount of dividends or income paid such person during the assessment year. *(1913 c. 720.)*

The object of this paragraph is to prevent double taxation. It means simply that any corporation owning stock or interest in any copartnership, corporation, joint stock company or association may deduct from its return of income that proportion of the dividends or income upon which income taxes have already been paid. If the copartnership or corporation does not report the name and address of the persons owning stocks or interest and the amount of dividends or income paid, the deductions cannot be allowed. The reports of copartnerships will be made to the income tax assessors. Corporations will report to the tax commission.

To constitute an assessment within the meaning of the statute there must be an assessment or levy of a tax because of the existence of the fund as income. Passing upon the taxability of the surplus in the hands of a company by the tax commission did not constitute an assessment of such surplus within the meaning of Ses. 1087m—3 (e). *State ex rel. Sallie F. Moon Company vs. Wisconsin Tax Commission,* 166 Wis. 287. *Van Dyke vs. City of Milwaukee,* 159 Wis. 460. *State ex rel. Columbia Construction Co. vs. Wisconsin Tax Commission,* 166 Wis. 369.

Bank Dividends

(g) Dividends received from state banks, national banks, mutual savings banks and trust companies subject to taxation by this state. *(1913 c. 615.)*

See notes to sections 1087m—4 (k) and 1087m—5—2.

Profits of Cooperative Associations

(h) Amounts distributed to patrons in any year, in proportion to their patronage of the same year, by any corporation, joint stock company or association doing business on a cooperative basis (hereinafter called "company"), whether organized under chapter 86 or otherwise, shall be returned as income or receipts by said patrons but may be deducted by such company as cost, purchase price or refunds; provided that no such deduction shall be made for amounts distributed to the stockholders or owners of such company in proportion to their stock or ownership, nor for amounts retained by such company and subject to distribution in proportion to stock or ownership as distinguished from patronage. *(1915 c. 252.)*

This provision recognizes the familiar principle that only so much of the earnings of a corporation as are distributed to stockholders in proportion to their holdings can be considered as dividends. Profits distributed in proportion to patronage represent additional payment for material and are deductible as such by the company paying the same but should be reported as additional price of product sold by the patrons receiving the same.

(i) Contributions or gifts actually made within the year to corporations or associations organized and operated exclusively for religious, charitable, scientific, or educational purposes, or to societies for the prevention of cruelty to children or animals, no part of the net income of which inures to the benefit of any private stockholder or individual, to an amount not in excess of fifteen per centum of the taxpayer's taxable net income as computed without the benefit of this paragraph. *(1919 c. 147.)*

While the above subsection allows as deductions, gifts and contributions, such deductions by no means include all gifts and contributions, but are limited:

1. To contributions and gifts made to corporations or associations. This limitation excludes gifts to individuals.

2. To gifts and contributions to corporations or associations organized exclusively for religious, charitable, scientific or educational purposes. This limitation excludes gifts made to business organizations, such as clubs, trade associations, baseball or other pleasure associations, etc. The purpose of the corporations or associations receiving the gifts should be inquired into in all cases to ascertain whether or not they are organized exclusively for the purposes set forth in the act.

3. To such gifts or contributions as are made to corporations or organizations, none of whose profits inure to the benefit of any private stockholder or individual. This means that all the income of the recipient of the gifts must be devoted to religious, charitable, scientific or educational purposes.

4. The aggregate amount of the gifts allowed to any one person as deductions must not exceed 15% of the net income of the taxpayer claiming such deduction.

DEDUCTIONS ALLOWED TO INDIVIDUALS

SECTION 1087m—4. Persons other than corporations, joint stock companies or associations, in reporting incomes for purposes of taxation shall be allowed the following deductions:

Wages and Salaries

(a) Payments made within the year for wages of employees and a reasonable allowance for services of copartners or members of a firm actually rendered in producing such income. But no deductions shall be made for any amount paid for personal services unless there be reported the name and address and amount paid each such employe or copartner to whom a sum of seven hundred dollars or more shall have been paid during the assessment year.

See note to section 1087m—3 (a).

The deductions authorized by this section are limited to wages and salaries paid for services rendered in producing the income reported. Compensation paid to domestic servants, chauffeurs, family physicians, and for like purposes, cannot be allowed as deductions. Such expenses are of a personal character and are presumed to be covered by the exemptions allowed. Members of a partnership are entitled to a reasonable allowance for their services to the firm but the amount should be definitely fixed in advance.

Ordinary and necessary expenses

(aa) The ordinary and necessary expenses actually paid within the year in carrying on the profession, occupation or business from which the income is derived, including a reasonable allowance for depreciation by use, wear and tear of the property from which the income is derived, and in the case of mines and quarries an allowance for depletion of ores and other natural deposits on the basis of their actual original cost in cash or the equivalent of cash. (1913 c. 720.)

See note to section 1087m—3 (b).

Losses

(b) Losses during the year and not compensated for by insurance or otherwise, provided that no loss resulting from the operation of business or the ownership of property may be al-

2

lowed as a deduction unless the income which might be derived from such business or property would be subject to taxation under this act. *(1919 c. 275.)*

See note to section 1087m—3 (e).

As elsewhere in the income tax law the deductions authorized by the two preceding subdivisions are confined to expenses incurred or losses sustained in connection with the business or property producing the income. Claims for depreciation or loss of property having no relation to the business carried on or the property employed therein are not allowable. This rule applies to all articles of luxury and ornament and other property used by the taxpayer for personal or family comfort or convenience.

As the estimated rental value of residence property is no longer taxable as income, the carrying charges thereon such as taxes, insurance, depreciation and repairs can not be allowed as deductions. Alimony paid to a divorced wife is in the nature of a division of property, and not being an expense incurred in producing the income reported is not an allowable deduction to the husband, nor income taxable to the wife. *Gould vs. Gould,* 245 U. S. 151.

No deduction can be allowed for depreciation or loss of mercantile stocks. The merchant is authorized to deduct the full cost of goods when purchased and if the stock depreciates in value thereafter the loss will be reflected in the reduced inventory at the end of the year or in the reduced price received therefor when sold. The same principle governs and the same rule applies in case of farm animals. The only expense incurred in connection with live stock raised by the owner is for their feed and care and these items are deductible as they accrue.

The cost of stock purchased for resale is a proper deduction but when once allowed no additional deduction for depreciation or loss is permissible. Stock purchased for breeding purposes or as a permanent addition to the herd may be regarded as capital investment and if the cost is not deducted at the time of purchase the owner may claim deduction in case of subsequent injury to or loss of such stock. See Federal Income Tax Service, Rules 215 to 222.

A person cultivating or operating a farm for recreation or pleasure on a basis other than the recognized principles of commercial farming, resulting in a loss from year to year, is not regarded as a farmer. In such cases if the expenses incurred in connection with the farm exceed the receipts therefrom, the proceeds from the sale of products should be ignored in making the assessment and the expenses incurred therein disallowed as personal expenses not subject to deduction from income derived from other sources. Income Tax Service, Rule 223, T. D. 2153.

Dividends

(c) Dividends or incomes received by any person from stocks or interest in any copartnership, corporation, joint stock company or association, the income of which shall have been assessed under the provisions of this act; provided that when only part of the income of any copartnership, corporation, joint stock company or association shall have been assessed under this act only a corresponding part of the dividends or income received therefrom shall be deducted, and provided, further, that said copartnership, corporation, joint stock company or association report the name and address of each person owning stock or having such interest and the amount of dividends or income paid to such person during the assessment year. (1913 c. 720.)

When only part of the income of a corporation is taxed in this state a stockholder should be allowed a proportionate and not a total deduction of dividends in computing the amount of his taxable income. *Van Dyke vs. City of Milwaukee*, 159 Wis. 460. *State ex rel. Columbia Construction Co. vs. Wisconsin Tax Commission*, 166 Wis. 369.

See note to section 1087m—3 (c).

No deduction is allowable from profits derived from the sale of corporate stock resulting from the existence of a surplus which has been taxed to the corporation, for the reason that the purchaser of the stock will be entitled to such deduction when the surplus is distributed in the form of dividends.

Interest on indebtedness

(d) Interest paid within the year on existing indebtedness; provided, the debtor reports the amount so paid, the form of the indebtedness, together with the name and address of the creditor.

Interest paid cannot be allowed as a deduction unless this section is strictly complied with.

Pensions

(g) Pensions received from the United States.

Taxes

(h) Taxes upon the property or business from which the income hereby is derived paid by such persons during the year other than inheritance taxes, including therein taxes imposed by the United States government as income, excess profits and war profits taxes. *(1919 c. 435.)*

Taxes paid on unproductive property are not allowable deductions. *State ex rel. Hickox vs. Widule,* 166 Wis. 113.

See note to section 1087m—3d.

Inheritances

(i) All inheritances, devises, bequests and gifts received during the year. *(1915 c. 253.)*

The effect of the 1915 amendment to this section is to exempt inheritances, devises, bequests and gifts from the income tax. The fact that they are enumerated under the head of deductions implies that they should be included in the return of income. The legislature could not have intended to allow the deduction of these additions to capital from income derived from other sources.

It should be borne in mind that it is only the corpus of the legacies or gifts, according to their value at the death of the testator or donor, which is subject to the inheritance tax and exempt from the income tax, and not the profits or income derived therefrom. All income from trust and life estates accruing subsequent to the death of the testator or intestate is taxable as such, and an assessment thereof to the fiduciary was sustained in *State ex rel. Hickox v. Widule,* 166 Wis. 113.

Ch. 318, Laws of 1917, expressly provides that such income shall not be exempt from income tax.

Whenever a transfer of property is made upon which there is, or in any contingency there may be, a tax imposed, such property shall be appraised at its clear market value immediately upon the transfer or as soon thereafter as practicable. The value of every future or limited estate, income, interest, or annuity dependent upon any life or lives in being, shall be determined by the rule, method, and standard of mortality and value employed by the commissioner of insurance in ascertaining the value of policies of life insurance and annuities for the determination of liabilities of life insurance companies, except that the rate of interest for making such computation shall be five per cent per annum. The tax so determined shall be construed to be upon the transfer of a proportion of the principal or corpus of the estate equal to the present value of such future or limited estate, income, interest, or annuity, and not upon any earnings or income of said property produced after death, *and such earnings or income shall not be exempt from the income tax.* Such tax shall be due and payable forthwith. *(1917 c. 318.)*

Life Insurance

(j) All insurance received by any person or persons in payment of a death claim by any insurance company, fraternal benefit society or other insurer. But endowment or other insurance paid to the insured in his lifetime shall be taxable upon the excess received over the amount paid for the insurance. *(1915 c. 253.)*

By chapter 253, laws of 1915, all insurance received on the payment of a death claim was withdrawn from the operation of the income tax law and made subject to inheritance taxes. But the proceeds of endowment policies paid to the insured during his lifetime are taxable as income to the extent that the insurance received exceeds the premiums paid. In other words the income tax applies to the profit element of the transaction.

Bank Dividends

(k) Dividends received from state banks, national banks, mutual savings banks and trust companies subject to taxation by this state. *(1913 c. 615.)*

The right of deduction conferred by this section is limited to dividends from banks "subject to taxation by this state." Dividends received by residents of Wisconsin from banks without the state should be returned as income and are not subject to deduction.

See note to section 1087m—5. 2.

(l) Contributions or gifts actually made within the year to corporations or associations organized and operated exclusively for religious, charitable, scientific, or educational purposes, or to societies for the prevention of cruelty to children or animals, no part of the net income of which inures to the benefit of any private stockholder or individual, to an amount not in excess of fifteen per centum of the taxpayer's taxable net income as computed without the benefit of this paragraph. *(1919 c. 147.)*

Note to section 1087m—31.

EXEMPTIONS

Exemptions to individuals

SECTION 1087m—5. 1. There shall be exempt from taxation under this act income as follows, to wit:

(a) To an individual income up to and including eight hundred dollars;

(b) To husband and wife twelve hundred dollars;

(c) For each child under the age of eighteen years, two hundred dollars;

(d) For each additional person, who is actually supported by and entirely dependent upon the taxpayer for his support, two hundred dollars. *(1913 c. 720.)*

The burden of proof rests on the person claiming exemption under (d) above to show that the person on account of whom he is claiming $200 additional exemption is not only "actually supported by" him but is also "entirely dependent upon" him.

Nonresidents, firms, corporations, etc. Income of wife and children

(e) The aforesaid exemption shall not apply to incomes derived from sources within the state by nonresidents thereof, nor to copartnerships, corporations, joint stock companies nor associations. In computing said exemptions and the amounts of taxes payable by persons residing together as members of a family, the income of the wife and the income of each child under eighteen years of age shall be added to that of the husband or father, or if he be not living, to that of the head of the family and assessed to him. The taxes levied thereon shall be payable by such husband or head of the family, but if not paid by him may be enforced against any person whose income is included in the assessment. *(1913 c. 720.)*

The above exemptions are based on the family unit, graduated according to the number of members and the estimated cost of maintaining a family "on the lowest scale of decent subsistence."

As such they are self-explanatory except as to the date when the exemption shall attach in case of the marriage, birth or death of a member of the family during the year.

In furtherance of the policy of the law and in the absence of a statutory guide in this respect the tax commission has ruled:

(1) That in case of the birth or death of a member of the family during the income year full exemption shall be allowed for the newborn or deceased member.

(2) That no exemption shall be allowed for minor children who attain the age of 18 during the income year, nor for children over 18 although supported by the parents unless incapable of supporting themselves from physical or mental infirmity.

(3) That all income received by minor children over 18 years of age shall be separately assessed to them and the full $800 exemption allowed.

(4) That in case of marriage or divorce during the year the full exemption for husband and wife shall be allowed to the husband when the wife has no separate income, but

(5) If both husband and wife have separate incomes the income of the wife prior to the date of marriage shall be separately assessed to her, subject to such part of the $800 exemption prescribed for individuals as the part of the year prior to marriage bears to the entire year.

(6) That the income of the husband for the entire year plus the income received by the wife subsequent to marriage shall be assessed to him subject to such part of the $800 exemption prescribed for individuals as that part of the year prior to date of marriage bears to the total year, plus such a part of the exemption prescribed for husband and wife as that part of the year subsequent to marriage bears to the entire year.

Banking, religious, educational, scientific, and benevolent associations

SECTION 1087m—5. 2. Income of state banks, national banks, mutual savings banks, trust companies and building and loan associations and of all religious, scientific, educational, benevolent or other corporations or associations of individuals not organized or conducted for pecuniary profit. *(1913 c. 615.)*

In the case of *National Bank v. Owensboro*, 173 U. S. 664, it was held that national banks can only be taxed in the manner authorized by Congress; that is, by assessment of the stock as property to the individual shareholders. As state banks are in direct competition with national banks and own property of the same character, consistency requires that they be taxed in the same manner. Moreover if the income of banks were assessed, the tax thereon would be subject to offset by the stock tax under section 1087m—26 of the statutes. For these reasons the legislature concluded to exclude banks from the operation of the income tax law altogether.

Where an educational corporation organized to conduct a private enterprise on the plan of a profit sharing corporation with capital stock owned by shareholders receives from its business an annual income in excess of its expenses and applies the excess to improving its properties, thus enhancing the value of the holdings to the stockholders, its income is not exempt from taxation under subsection 2, sec. 1087m—5 of the statutes. *St. Johns Military Academy vs. Larson*, 168 Wis. 357.

Incomes from public service corporations

SECTION 1087m—5. 3. Incomes derived from property and privileges by persons now required by law to pay taxes or license fees directly into the treasury of the state in lieu of taxes, and such persons shall continue to pay taxes and license fees as heretofore.

This section seems to exempt from the payment of income tax:

Railroad companies
Palace and sleeping car companies
Freight line and equipment companies
Express companies
Street railway companies including connected electric light, heat and power companies
Telegraph companies
Fire insurance companies
Life insurance companies
Accident, surety, etc. companies
Telephone companies
Title guaranty companies
Conservation and regulation companies.

Telephone and insurance companies are taxed upon their gross earnings under the license system. In the assessment of state wide public service companies the franchise element is required to be included, and the earnings or income are taken into account in determining their value. For that reason they have been exempted from the income tax. This exemption does not extend to local utilities, such as water, light, heat and power companies except when owned and operated in connection with street railways.

Public funds

SECTION 1087m—5. 4. Income received by the United States, the state and all counties, cities, villages, school districts or other political units of this state.

RATES

Rates for individuals

SECTION 1087m—6. 1. The tax to be assessed, levied and collected upon the incomes of all persons, except as otherwise provided by law, after making such deductions and exemptions as are hereinbefore allowed, shall be computed at the following rates, to wit:

(a) On the first one thousand dollars of taxable income or any part thereof, at the rate of one per cent;

(b) On the second one thousand dollars or any part thereof, one and one-fourth per cent;

(c) On the third one thousand dollars or any part thereof, one and one-half per cent;

(d) On the fourth one thousand dollars or any part thereof, one and three-fourths per cent;

(e) On the fifth one thousand dollars or any part thereof, two per cent;

(f) On the sixth one thousand dollars or any part thereof, two and one-half per cent;

(g) On the seventh one thousand dollars or any part thereof, three per cent;

(h) On the eighth one thousand dollars or any part thereof, three and one-half per cent;

(i) On the ninth one thousand dollars or any part thereof, four per cent;

(j) On the tenth one thousand dollars or any part thereof, four and one-half per cent;

(k) On the eleventh one thousand dollars or any part thereof, five per cent;

(l) On the twelfth one thousand dollars or any part thereof, five and one-half per cent;

(m) On any sum of taxable income in excess of twelve thousand dollars, six per cent.

Rates for corporations

SECTION 1087m—6. 2. The taxes to be assessed, levied and collected upon the incomes of corporations, joint stock companies or associations, after making such deductions and exemptions as hereinbefore allowed, shall be computed at the following rates, to wit:

On the first $1,000 of taxable income or any part thereof..2%
On the second $1,000 of taxable income or any part thereof..2½
On the third $1,000 of taxable income or any part thereof..3
On the fourth $1,000 of taxable income or any part thereof..3½
On the fifth $1,000 of taxable income or any part thereof..4
On the sixth $1,000 of taxable income or any part thereof..5
On the seventh $1,000 of taxable income or any part thereof.6
On all taxable income in excess of $7,000 6
   (1913 c. 720.)

The following tables which apply only to even thousands, may be helpful in computing rates:

CORPORATIONS

Taxable Income	Rate per cent	Tax	Total income taxed	Total tax	True rate on whole amount in even thousands
1st $1,000...............	2	$20.00	$1,000	$20.00	2%
2nd $1,000...............	2½	25.00	2,000	45.00	2.25
3rd $1,000...............	3	30.00	3,000	75.00	2.5
4th $1,000...............	3½	35.00	4,000	110.00	2.75
5th $1,000...............	4	40.00	5,000	150.00	3.
6th $1,000...............	5	50.00	6,000	200.00	3.3333
7th $1,000...............	6	60.00	7,000	260.00	3.7143
8th $1,000...............	6	60.00	8,000	320.00	4.
9th $1,000...............	6	60.00	9,000	380.00	4.2222
10th $1,000...............	6	60.00	10,000	440.00	4.4
15th $1,000...............	6	60.00	15,000	740.00	4.9333
20th $1,000...............	6	60.00	20,000	1,040.00	5.2

INDIVIDUALS

	Taxable Income	Rate per cent	Tax	Total income taxed	Total tax	True rate on whole amount
1st...........	$1,000	1	$10.00	$1,000	$10.00	1%
2nd...........	1,000	1¼	12.50	2,000	22.50	1.125
3rd...........	1,000	1½	15.00	3,000	37.50	1.25
4th...........	1,000	1¾	17.50	4,000	55.00	1.375
5th...........	1,000	2	20.00	5,000	75.00	1.5
6th...........	1,000	2½	25.00	6,000	100.00	1.6667
7th...........	1,000	3	30.00	7,000	130.00	1.8571
8th...........	1,000	3½	35.00	8,000	165.00	2.0625
9th...........	1,000	4	40.00	9,000	205.00	2.2778
10th...........	1,000	4½	45.00	10,000	250.00	2.5
11th...........	1,000	5	50.00	11,000	300.00	2.7273
12th...........	1,000	5½	55.00	12,000	355.00	2.9582
13th...........	1,000	6	60.00	13,000	415.00	3.1923
15th...........	1,000	6	60.00	15,000	535.00	3.5667
20th...........	1,000	6	60.00	20,000	835.00	4.175

PART II

ADMINISTRATION

Division of state into assessment districts

SECTION 1087m—8. 1. The state shall be divided into assessment districts by the state tax commission, but in no instance shall a county be divided.

In accordance with this authority the tax commission has made the following division of the state into forty districts:

No. of district	No. of district
1. Kenosha	22. Calumet, Manitowoc
2. Racine	23. Door, Kewaunee
3. Walworth	24. Brown, Oconto
4. Rock	25. Outagamie, Waupaca
5. Green, Lafayette	26. Portage, Wood
6. Grant, Iowa	27. Clark, Jackson
7. Dane	28. Buffalo, Pepin, Trempealeau
8. Jefferson	29. Pierce, St. Croix
9. Waukesha	30. Chippewa, Barron
10. Milwaukee	31. Marathon
11. Ozaukee, Washington	32. Shawano, Langlade
12. Dodge	33. Florence, Forest, Marinette
13. Columbia, Marquette	34. Oneida, Vilas, Lincoln
14. Sauk	35. Price, Taylor
15. Crawford, Richland	36. Rusk, Sawyer
16. La Crosse	37. Burnett, Polk
17. Adams, Juneau	38. Douglas, Washburn
19. Winnebago, Waushara	39. Ashland, Bayfield, Iron
20. Fond du Lac, Green Lake	40. Dunn, Eau Claire
21. Sheboygan	41. Monroe, Vernon

Assessors of incomes; how appointed

SECTION 1087m—8. 2. Not less than thirty days prior to the first of March, 1912, there shall be selected and appointed by the state tax commission an assessor of incomes for each assessment district in the state, who shall hold office for a term of three years unless sooner removed as hereinafter provided. Such assessor shall be a citizen and an elector of this state, but need not be a resident of the district in which he is appointed to serve; provided, however, that so far as practicable, preference shall be given in making such appointments to residents of the districts.

The office of assessor of incomes is not a county, city, town or village office, and appointments thereto may be made by state authority without conflict with the home rule clause of the constitution. Income Tax Cases, 148 Wis. 456. Subject to civil service requirements, all citizens and electors of the state are eligible to the office of assessor of incomes, but preference is required to be given to residents of the district to be served. All assessors of incomes heretofore appointed have been residents of their respective districts.

Assessors of incomes; how transferred or removed

SECTION 1087m—8. 3. The tax commission may in its discretion transfer any assessor of incomes from one district to another and may remove any assessor of incomes or his deputy from office.

Oath to be taken and filed

SECTION 1087m—8. 4. Before entering upon his duties such assessor of incomes shall subscribe to the constitutional oath and file the same in the office of the secretary of state. He shall be under the direction and control of the state tax commission, and shall make such reports to the commission, to the county board of review and the county board of supervisors, and perform such other duties, as the commission shall direct. *(1913 c. 443.)*

Deputies and assistants

SECTION 1087m—8. 5. The state tax commission may authorize any assessor of incomes to appoint such deputies and other assistants as may be required for the proper performance of his duties. Such deputies shall qualify in like manner and possess the same powers as the assessor.

Salaries and expenses

SECTION 1087m—9. 1. The salaries of the assessors of incomes and their deputies and assistants shall be fixed by the state tax commission, but such salaries, together with the expenses of such assessors and their deputies and assistants, shall not in any year exceed in amount five cents for every thousand dollars of the valuation of all property as fixed by the tax commission in the state assessment of the preceding year. The assessor shall be furnished all necessary printing, stationery, postage and office equipment, and he and his deputies shall be entitled to receive their actual necessary expenses incurred in the performance of their duties. The salaries of the assessor and his assistants, and all such expenditures shall be audited and paid out of the state treasury in the same manner as other similar salaries and state expenses are audited and paid.

2. The county board of each county in which the assessor of incomes has an office shall provide at the expense of the county a suitable room or rooms in the courthouse or other convenient building at the county seat for the use of such assessor. If any county shall fail or refuse to furnish suitable quarters for the use of the assessor of incomes as herein provided the tax commission may procure such quarters at the expense of the county primarily responsible therefor. *(1913 c. 487.)*

Under the foregoing provision, assessors of incomes are provided with offices at the expense of the county. The terms "suitable rooms" or "quarters" mean rooms appropriate and adequate to the business of the office and include light and heat. Without light and heat such rooms would be wholly unsuitable. Whether the words include office equipment is not so certain, but as many counties have provided assessors of incomes with appropriate equipment, and as such equipment can be supplied by counties at a saving of expense, it is believed that the term "office rooms" or "quarters" ought to be given a liberal construction, and that the offices of all the assessors of incomes ought to be equipped at the counties' expense with whatever is required in the way of office furniture, filing cases, etc.

When and by whom assessments made

SECTION 1087m—10. 1. The state tax commission and the assessors of incomes shall annually on the first day of January, or as soon thereafter as practicable, proceed to assess as hereinafter provided every income received during the preceding calendar year liable to taxation under the provisions of this act. Liability to taxation for income which follows the residence of the recipient in the case of persons moving into or out of the state shall be determined by the residence of such person on the thirty-first day of December of the income year, and liability to taxation on like income in the case of corporations which have been created or dissolved before assessment shall be determined by the status of such corporation on the same date. The assessment of corporations, joint stock companies and associations shall be made by the state tax commission, and the assessment of persons other than corporations, joint stock companies and associations shall be by the county assessor of incomes. *(1913 c. 720.)*

Powers of tax commission and assessors of incomes

SECTION 1087m—10. 2. In the performance of such duty the state tax commission and the county assessors of incomes shall respectively possess all powers now or hereafter granted by law to the state tax commission or assessors in the assessment of personal property and also the power to estimate incomes.

Among the powers conferred by this section are those set forth in section 1056 of the Revised Statutes authorizing the assessor to examine persons under oath and to require them to make sworn statements. The "power to estimate incomes" is the so-called "doomage power."

A doomage assessment does not exempt the taxpayer doomed from the penalties provided by law for failure to make a return.

Returns by corporations

SECTION 1087m—10. 3. Every corporation, joint stock company or association, whether taxable under this act or not, shall furnish to the tax commission a true and accurate statement at such time, in such manner and form and setting forth such facts as said commission shall deem necessary to enforce the provisions of this act. Such statement shall be made upon the oath or affirmation of the president, vice president or other principal officer and the treasurer of said corporation, joint stock company or association.

Returns by individuals

SECTION 1087m—10. 4. Whenever in the judgment of the assessor of incomes any person in his district other than a corporation, joint stock company or association shall be subject to an income tax under the provisions of this act, he shall require such person to make report at such time and in such manner and form as the tax commission may prescribe, specifying particularly among other items the amount of income received from services, unsecured notes, mortgages, bonds, stocks and real estate, the amount of income received by his wife and each child under eighteen years of age residing together with him as members of the family and such other information as the commission shall deem necessary to enforce the provisions of this act. (1913 c. 720.)

All unmarried persons who have a gross annual income of over $800 and all married persons who have a gross annual income of over $1,200 should make a return whether notified by the assessor of incomes to do so or not.

All persons who are notified to make return of income by the assessor of incomes should comply with the notice regardless of the amount of their incomes.

Returns by guardians, trustees, etc.

SECTION 1087m—10. 5. Every guardian, trustee, executor, administrator, agent or receiver, and every other person or corporation acting in a fiduciary capacity shall make and render to the assessor of incomes of the district in which such representative resides, a verified list or return of the amount of income received by him for such person, ward or beneficiary, together with all income received by the ward, beneficiary, deceased or incompetent person whom he represents or succeeds during the year covered by the return and shall be liable to assessment and taxation therefor, subject to the deductions and exemptions provided in this chapter; provided, that such deductions or exemptions have not been claimed by or for such person, ward or beneficiary in another capacity. The return so made shall be signed by the person rendering it, and by the president or secretary thereof, if a corporation. Every person subject to an income tax in his representative capacity under this subdivision shall have all of the remedies and rights of reimbursement for any tax assessed against or paid by him in such capacity prescribed by section 1044a of the statutes. *(1913 c. 720.)*

Dividends derived from stocks and interest derived from notes, mortgages, etc., received by a resident trustee (individual or corporate) as a gain or profit from securities constituting the trust fund are taxable as income in this state even though the person entitled to the enjoyment thereof and to whom they must be paid over is a nonresident and also a cotrustee, and even though two of the trustees reside without the state. The resident trustee, in such a case, in whose custody the securities are, and to whom the dividends and interest are paid, must be deemed the recipient of such income within the meaning of subdivision 3, Sec. 1087m—2. *State ex rel. Hickox vs. Widule,* 166 Wis. 113. *State ex rel. Wisconsin Trust Co. vs. Widule,* 156 Wis. 121.

Expenses incurred in the probate of an estate, such as administrators', executors' and attorneys' fees and inheritance taxes are not proper deductions in computing annual income. Inheritance taxes are excluded by the express letter of the statute and the other expenses have no relation to the income of the current year. The services of executors, administrators, attorneys and appraisers mainly relate to the adjustment of claims, devolution of title and conservation of the property of the estate and are therefore proper charges against the corpus. Such expenses are denied by the Internal Revenue Department in administering the federal income tax law and the tax commission has repeatedly ruled that they are not allowable under the Wisconsin law. On the other hand if the executor or administrator continues the business of the deceased, all ordinary expenses incident to carrying on the business during the year are deductible to the same extent as if the business had been conducted by the former owner.

Where paid by guardians, etc.

5a. The income tax to be paid by guardians, trustees, agents or other persons or corporations acting in a fiduciary capacity shall, as to such income as follows the residence of the recipient, be paid in the district where the said guardian, trustee, agent or other fiduciary resides, if the ward, beneficiary or principal is a nonresident of the state of Wisconsin. If the ward, beneficiary or principal resides in the state of Wisconsin the tax upon all such income shall be paid in the district where the said ward, beneficiary or principal resides. *(1915 c. 408.)*

Returns by executors, etc. required before estate can be settled

5b. An executor, administrator, guardian or trustee applying to a court having jurisdiction for a discharge from his trust and a final settlement of his accounts, before his application shall be granted, shall file with the assessor of incomes of his county a return of all income received in his representative capacity during the time between the last preceding January first and the date of his application for discharge and also similar returns of income received during each of the three next preceding calendar years as have not theretofore been filed. Upon receipt of such returns the income tax assessor shall immediately determine the amount of income tax due or to become due from such executor, administrator, guardian, or trustee and certify the amount or amounts to the court in which the application for discharge is pending and the court shall thereupon enter an order directing the executor, administrator, trustee or guardian, as the case may be, to pay to the treasurer of the county in which such proceeding is pending the amount of tax, if any, found due by the assessor of incomes, and take his receipt therefor. The certificate of the assessor of incomes shall contain the names of the counties, towns, cities or villages entitled to the tax and the amount to which each is entitled and a copy thereof shall be filed with the treasurer of the county in which said court is located. Such receipt shall be evidence of the payment of the tax and shall be filed with the court before a final distribution of the estate is ordered, and the executor, administrator, or trustee is discharged. The county treasurer shall pay to the several treasurers of the state, county, town, city and village the portion of the tax each is entitled to at the time and in the manner delinquent income taxes are paid to him. The assessor of incomes shall enter all such assessments upon the assessment roll for the year in which the assessment is made, if practicable to do so, otherwise upon the assessment roll of the following year and shall enter thereon opposite each such assessment the words "Paid to the county treasurer by order of court." (1919 c. 386.)

In answer to numerous inquiries the tax commission has issued the following instructions to assessors of incomes relating to the assessment of executors, etc.

"(1) Executors, administrators, guardians and trustees are required to make return of all income received by them in their representative capacity for each calendar year during the existence of the trust. The return for the year of their appointment should also include the income received by the deceased or incompetent person whom they represent or succeed from the first of January preceding to the date of appointment. Under the foregoing amendment the return for the year in which the trust is terminated should cover the income from the first of January preceding to the date of final settlement. All such returns should be made on the regular blanks prescribed for executors, administrators, trustees and others acting in a fiduciary capacity. In case any such representative or the person whom he represents or succeeds shall have failed or omitted to make a return of the income received by him for either of the next three preceding years, he should make separate return of such income.

(2) The exemptions prescribed for individuals are based upon the family unit. In the ordinary course of probate of an estate the executor or administrator stands in the place of the former owner and the unity of the family is generally preserved. During this period, therefore, exemption should be measured by the family status. It follows that executors and administrators should be allowed the same exemptions for the year in which the deceased died which he might have claimed if he had survived. In subsequent years no exemption should be allowed for the deceased, but full exemption should be allowed for the succeeding head of the family and minors and dependent members thereof.

3

(3) As a general rule the tenure of guardians and trustees is more permanent and the family relation among the beneficiaries less frequent. In such cases when the return covers a full calendar year the statute seems to contemplate that exemptions should be allowed according to the status of the beneficiary as if he reported in his individual capacity. As the return for the year in which the trust is terminated covers only the income received from the first of January preceding to the date of final settlement, and the beneficiary must make return for the balance of the year, care should be exercised to avoid double exemption. In that event at the option of the beneficiary the fiduciary may claim exemption for him or the beneficiary may waive the exemption in the return made by the fiduciary and avail himself of it in his individual return. When the fiduciary claims exemption for the beneficiary and such exemption exceeds his share of the income reported, the unused portion of the exemption may be claimed by the beneficiary in making his individual return.

(4) Every assessor of incomes should require returns of all fiduciaries appointed by or acting under the jurisdiction of any court in his district, who may be liable for an income tax, preliminary to final settlement of their estates. He should assess the income as soon as the returns are received and certify the amount of the tax due thereon to the court having jurisdiction of the trust and mail a duplicate copy of such certificate to the county treasurer and enter the same on the income tax assessment roll in the manner prescribed by sec. 1087m—10. 5b.

Court may waive return, when

(5c) Returns of income required to be made by virtue of the next preceding subsection may be dispensed with by order of the court having jurisdiction in cases where it is clearly evident to the court that no income is due or to become due from the trust estate. *(1919 c. 419.)*

Should the court make an order dispensing with the return under the authority of subsection 5c and after the final settlement and distribution of the estate it shall be ascertained that taxable income had been received, the fiduciary is personally responsible for the tax. The court is not made a substitute for, but an aid to, the assessor of incomes. Any order dispensing with the return will be made at the risk of the fiduciary, and hence in all cases it is greatly to his interest to see to it that no such order is inadvertently made.

The certificate required by section 1087m—10.5b may be substantially in the following form:

CERTIFICATE

County Court— .... **County, Wisconsin**

In the Matter of the ....of ⎫
........................., Deceased. ⎰

I, the undersigned, assessor of incomes in and for ....
.... County, Wisconsin, hereby certify that
.... as ....
of the estate of ...., deceased, has made due return of all income received by him in his
representative capacity as required by Section 1087m—10.5b of
the Statutes (ch. 265, Laws of 1917 and ch. 386, Laws of 1919) ;
that I have carefully examined said return and find the amount
of income taxes due from him as ....of
said estate to be as follows:

$................on income received by him for current year,
$................on income received by him in 19
$................on income received by him in 19
$................on income received by him in 19

That said Estate is being administered in the County Court
of ....County, and the tax thereon
is payable to the treasurer of said county, to be distributed by
him in the following manner:

70% or $.........to be paid to the Treasurer of ....
20% or $.........to be retained by him for the County of.....
....
10% or $.........to be paid to Treasurer of State of Wisconsin. (Or)

That I have carefully examined the accounts of ....
.... as ....of the said estate
and that there is no income tax due from him in his representative capacity.
Dated this ....day of................, 19....
....
Assessor of Incomes,
..............................County, Wisconsin.

Penalty on assessor for questions unanswered

SECTION 1087m—10. 6. For each question unanswered the
assessor or deputy assessor, failing to present satisfactory cause
for such omission to the state tax commission, shall be subject to
a penalty of five dollars, and said penalty shall be deducted

from the compensation of said assessor or deputy assessor at the time such compensation is paid.

Additions and corrections to returns

SECTION 1087m—11. 1. Whenever evidence shall be produced before the state tax commission, which in the opinion of the commission, justifies the belief that in any one or more of the three next previous years the returns made by any corporation, joint stock company or association are incorrect, or are made with false or fraudulent intent, or when any corporation, joint stock company or association has failed or refused to make a return as required by law the state tax commission may require from every such corporation, joint stock company or association such further information with reference to its capital, income, losses, expenditures and business transactions as is. deemed expedient. Upon the information so required the state tax commission may make such additions or corrections to the assessment as are deemed true and just, such correction to be made in the next tax levy. Whenever the state tax commission shall so increase or make subject to tax any income, it shall give notice in writing to the person liable for the payment of the tax on said income of the amount of the assessment. Such notice may be served by registered mail.

Penalty on corporations for false or fraudulent return or failure to make return

SECTION 1087m—11. 2. In case any return made by any corporation, joint stock company or association is made with false or fraudulent intent or in case of a refusal or neglect to make a return as required by law, and an additional amount is discovered, the amount so discovered shall be subject to twice the original rate. The amount so added to the tax shall be collected at such time and in such manner as may be designated by the state tax commission.

In addition to the power to reassess corporations for taxes omitted in any of the three previous years, the tax commission is authorized, if not required, to tax the income at double the original rate. In the case of failure to make a return the tax commission may ''estimate'' the income and impose the double tax rate upon the income thus fixed.

This section gives the tax commission power to correct errors and reassess incomes of corporations which escaped taxation in former years but limits the time within which such corrections can be made to the three years immediately preceding. Income of this character which escaped taxation more than three years prior to the year of assessment cannot be reached under this statute but it does not follow that the taxes due thereon cannot be enforced at all. On the contrary it is well settled by decisions of the United States supreme court and of several states that such taxes can be collected by direct action against the taxpayer after the right to reassess has expired.

Dollar Savings Bank vs. United States, 86 U. S. 227;

Meredith vs. United States, 13 Peters 486;

United States vs. Chamberlain, 219 U. S. 250.

The same rule has been applied in several of the states, notably in California, Massachusetts, New York, and Connecticut, and is probably the general law.

When time for making returns may be extended

SECTION 1087m—11. 3. In case of neglect occasioned by the sickness or absence of an officer of any corporation, joint stock company or association required to make said return, or for other sufficient reason, the state tax commission may allow such further time for making and delivering such return as it may deem necessary, not to exceed thirty days.

Penalty on corporation for making false return, etc.

SECTION 1087m—11. 4. If any of the corporations, joint stock companies or associations aforesaid shall fail or refuse to make a return at the time or times hereinbefore specified in each year, or shall render a false or fraudulent return, such corporation, joint stock company or association shall be liable to a penalty of not less than one hundred dollars and not to exceed five thousand dollars at the discretion of the court.

Penalties on officers of corporations

SECTION 1087m—11. 5. Any officer of a corporation, joint stock company or association required by law to make, render, sign or verify any return who makes any false or fraudulent return or statement, with intent to defeat or evade the assessment required by this act to be made, shall upon conviction be fined not to exceed five hundred dollars or be imprisoned not to exceed one year, or both, at the discretion of the court, with the cost of prosecution.

Additions, corrections and reassessments of incomes of individuals

SECTION 1087m—12. 1. Whenever the assessor of incomes or the county board of review herein provided for shall have reason to believe that in any one or more of the three next previous years the returns made by any person other than a corporation, joint stock company, or association are incorrect or are made with false or fraudulent intent, or when any such person has failed or refused to make a return as required by law, the assessor or county board of review shall make such additions or corrections to the next assessment as he or they shall deem true and just. Whenever the assessor or the county board of review shall so increase or make subject to tax any income he or they shall give notice in writing to the person liable for the payment of the tax on said income of the amount of the assessment. Such notice may be served by registered mail.

This section provides the same method, for reassessing income taxes which have been omitted within three years by individuals as is set forth in the case of corporations in section 1087m—11, sub. 1, except that in the former case the reassessment is made by the tax commission while for individuals it is made by the assessor of incomes or the board of review.

See note 1087m—11. 2.

Penalty for false return by individual

SECTION 1087m—12. 2. In case any return made by any person other than a corporation, joint stock company or association is made with false or fraudulent intent, or in case of a refusal or neglect to make a return as required by law, and an additional amount is discovered, the amount so discovered shall be subject to twice the original rate.

Penalty on individual for making false return, etc.

SECTION 1087m—12. 3. Any person, other than a corporation, joint stock company or association who fails or refuses to make a return at the time hereinbefore specified in each year or shall render a false or fraudulent return shall upon conviction be fined not to exceed five hundred dollars, or be imprisoned not to exceed one year, or both, at the discretion of the court, together with the cost of prosecution.

APPEAL AND REVIEW

Appeal by corporation

SECTION 1087m—13. Any corporation, joint stock company or association subject to assessment by the state tax commission, feeling aggrieved by the decision of said commission regarding the assessment of its income, shall be granted the same rights of hearing and appeal as are now granted corporations assessed by said commission.

The "hearing and appeal" referred to in this section is in the nature of a review or rehearing before the tax commission as to the amount of income on which the corporation should be taxed. The section does not refer to proceedings in court nor does it authorize an action against the state to recover taxes unlawfully levied, as in the case of steam railroads. Relief from the levy or collection of an unlawful income tax must be sought under subdivision 4 of section 1087m—22 and sections 1164 and 1210g of the statutes. See *Montreal Mining Co. vs. State,* 155 Wis. 245.

Board of review—appointment and compensation

SECTION 1087m—14. The state tax commission shall appoint three resident taxpayers of each county to serve as a county board of review. *(1913 c. 772.)*

Duties of county clerk as clerk of board of review

SECTION 1087m—15. The county clerk shall be clerk of such board, and shall keep an accurate record of all proceedings thereof, including a correct record of all changes in the assessment rolls made by the board. The county clerk shall take full minutes of all evidence given before the board; provided, however, that the board, with the approval of the assessor of incomes, may in cases where they deem it advisable, employ a stenographic reporter to take such evidence in shorthand, and extend the same in typewritten form. The county clerk shall preserve in his office a record of all such proceedings, minutes and evidence taken, and all documentary evidence offered. The stenographer shall be paid by the state, such payment to be charged to the proper appropriation for the tax commission, but the board may, in its discretion, charge the expenses to the complaining party or parties appearing before the board. *(1913 c. 772.)*

Board of Review shall meet last Monday of July

SECTION 1087m—16. 1. The county board of review of each county, constituting an assessment district, shall meet annually on the last Monday of July at ten o'clock a. m. at the courthouse in said county to hear complaints and to review the assessments of income made by the assessor. A majority shall constitute a quorum.

Date of meeting in districts comprising more than one county

2. In assessment districts composed of more than one county the board of review of the county designated by the assessor of incomes shall meet as provided above and the board of review of each remaining county of the district shall meet as soon thereafter as is possible for the assessor of incomes to be present. The date of such meeting shall be fixed by the assessor of incomes.

Notice of meeting to be published

3. Notice of the annual meeting of each county board of review shall be published in a newspaper of the county at least one week previous to such meeting.

This section does not specify by whom the notice of the meeting of the board of review shall be signed. In the absence of such direction the tax commission has ruled that it shall be signed by the assessor of incomes. The following form of notice is recommended for the purpose:

Notice is hereby given that the income tax board of review in and for .... County will meet at the courthouse in the city of ...., on the .... day of July 19 ...., at 10 o'clock in the forenoon, for the purpose of examining the income tax assessment roll and of considering complaints of aggrieved taxpayers and performing such other duties as are imposed upon it by law.

Dated at ....this........day of July, 19....

....

Assessor of Incomes in and
for ....County.

Adjournments

4. The board may adjourn from day to day, and from time to time, until its business is completed, but no adjournment other than from day to day shall be had except upon written request and for satisfactory cause shown.

Attendance of witnesses and production of books and papers

5. Attendance of witnesses and the production of books and papers before said board may be compelled by subpoena, issued by the clerk thereof, a justice of the peace or a court commissioner.

Duties of board of review

SECTION 1087m—17. 1. The board shall hear and examine, and permit the assessor to examine, any aggrieved or other person upon oath who shall appear before it in relation to any assessment or omission of income, and may increase or lessen the amount of any income assessed, if satisfied from the evidence submitted and the statements of the assessor, that such change should be made.

The powers and duties of income tax boards of review are substantially the same as those prescribed by section 1061 of the statutes relating to the property tax. Their principal duty is to pass upon disputed facts and not to modify or suspend any provision of the income tax law or the regulations prescribed for the administration thereof. While the reason for such laws and regulations may not be apparent in all cases, they were framed with reference to their effect on the administration of the law as a whole and are generally observed in making assessments. The failure of individual boards of review to be governed by them will inevitably destroy the uniformity between taxpayers which it is the policy of the law to maintain.

Board must give notice of changes in assessment

2. The board shall not increase any assessments, nor assess any income not on the roll without notice in writing to the person liable for payment of the tax thereon, or his agent, if either be resident of the county, of such intention in time to appear and be heard before the board in relation thereto.

Objections to assessment must be made before board of review

SECTION 1087m—18. No person subject to assessment by the county assessor shall be allowed in any action or proceeding to question any assessment of income, unless objections thereto shall first have been presented to the county board of review in good faith and full disclosure made under oath of any and all income of such party liable to assessment.

Appeal may be taken to state tax commission

SECTION 1087m—19. 1. Any person dissatisfied with any determination of the county board of review may appeal within twenty days to the state tax commission, to whom a copy of the record of the board shall be certified, together with all evidence or a copy thereof, relating to such assessment.

An income tax assessor if dissatisfied with the decision of the board of review of income tax assessments, has the right to appeal therefrom to the state tax commission. *State ex rel. Wickham vs. Nygaard,* 159 Wis. 396.

The remedy of appeal to the state tax commission by a person dissatisfied with any determination of the county board of review in respect to the assessment of his income is not exclusive. Nor is such an appeal a condition precedent to the right to maintain an action for the recovery of illegal income taxes paid under protest. Such action may be maintained under subdivision (4), Sec. 1087m—22 and Sec. 1164. *Horlick vs. Town of Mt. Pleasant,* 161 Wis. 366. *Field vs. Milwaukee,* 161 Wis. 393.

Tax commission may review assessments **on appeal**

2. The tax commission shall review such assessment from the record thus submitted and shall make necessary corrections and certify its conclusion to the county clerk, who shall duly notify the person liable for the tax and enter upon the assessment roll any change made by the commission.

APPORTIONMENT AND COLLECTION

Tax commission to compute and certify tax on corporations

SECTION 1087m—20. 1. The state tax commission shall complete the assessment of income for each corporation, joint stock company, and association on or before the fifteenth day of October in each year, and compute the tax thereon, and shall thereupon forthwith certify to each county clerk a statement of the assessment of each corporation, joint stock company and association in his county and the amount of tax levied against each.

Tax commission to make report

2. The state tax commission shall submit in their biennial report the amount of income tax collected for each county in the

state, and shall designate the several general classes of property from which the incomes were received, the cost to the state and each county for the administration of the law, and all such facts as shall be required to give a definite understanding of the financial operations of the law.

In compliance with this statute the tax commission has submitted the results of the administration of the law in its biennial report to the legislature. The following summary shows the results of the income tax for each assessment from 1912 to 1918, inclusive.

TABLE SHOWING INCOME TAX LEVY, CASH COLLECTIONS, OFFSETS AND DELINQUENTS FOR THE YEARS 1912 TO 1918 INCLUSIVE

Year	Total levy	Offsets	Cash collections	delinquent
Income of 1911, assessed in 1912, paid in 1913	$3,482,883.25	$1,609,711.02	$1,631,413.38	$241,758.85
Income of 1912, assessed in 1913, paid in 1914	4,085,147.56	1,897,974.05	1,935,846.54	251,326.97
Income of 1913, assessed in 1914, paid in 1915	4,145,676.48	1,987,904.52	2,002,212.53	155,559.43
Income of 1914, assessed in 1915, paid in 1916	3,837,370.04	1,825,641.62	1,906,441.69	105,286.73
Income of 1915, assessed in 1916, paid in 1917	5,328,442.96	2,211,606.89	2,988,766.66	128,069.41
Income of 1916, assessed in 1917, paid in 1918	9,482,620.13	3,807,435.67	6,037,719.19	137,465.27
Income of 1917, assessed in 1918, paid in 1919	11,784,151.34	4,707,187.96	6,951,482.70	125,480.68

By whom income tax of individuals to be computed

SECTION 1087m—21. 1. The tax upon the income of persons other than corporations, joint stock companies and associations shall be computed by the county clerk, assisted by the assessor of incomes and said clerk shall on or before November first, certify, excepting in cities of the first class, to each town, city and village clerk the names of all persons whose incomes are assessed in his own town, city or village, and the amount of tax levied against each such person, and such amount shall be entered by the town, city and village clerks in a separate column designated "income tax" upon the tax roll of the year, and shall be collected and paid as personal property taxes are now collected and paid.

2. The county clerk shall certify in a similar manner to the tax commissioner of each city of the first class located within the limits of the county and the tax commissioner shall proceed in the manner previously prescribed for the city clerk to make out the tax roll. *(1915 c. 335.)*

Where tax shall be assessed, levied and collected

SECTION 1087m—22. The place at which the income tax herein provided for shall be assessed, levied and collected shall be determined as follows:

1. In their return for purposes of assessment persons deriving incomes from within and without the state, or from more than one political subdivision of the state, shall make a separate accounting of the income derived from without the state and from each political subdivision of the state in such form and manner as the tax commission may prescribe.

Much confusion has arisen from the failure of taxpayers to furnish the necessary data for apportioning income taxes under this section. Where a taxpayer receives income from different assessment districts within the state, the method of apportionment is substantially the same as where income is derived from within and without the state. See note to section 1087m—2. 3. Persons doing business in different assessment districts within the state should carefully report (1) the total amount of tangible property employed in carrying on the business and the amount located in each assessment district; (2) the total amount of business transacted during the year in all districts and the amount in each particular district, preferably expressed in gross receipts; (3) the factory cost of (a) goods sold, and (b) goods manufactured in all districts and in each separate district. It should be borne in mind that it is the town, city or village in which the property is located or business transacted which is entitled to the tax, and the name of such municipality should be carefully given in addition to the post-office address.

Assessment of income derived from different localities

SECTION 1087m—22. 2. The entire taxable income of every person deriving income from within and without the state or from within different political subdivisions of the state, when such person resides within the state, shall be combined and aggregated for the purpose of determining the proper exemptions and proper rate of taxation. The taxable income so computed shall be assessed, and taxes at such rate shall be paid, in the several towns, cities and villages in proportion to the respective amounts of income derived from each, counting that part of the income derived from without the state when taxable as having been derived from the town, city or village in which said person resides.

Where income tax of nonresidents to be paid

SECTION 1087m—22. 3. The income tax of every nonresident of this state shall be paid in the taxing district from which the income is derived. When such income is derived from more than one taxing district of the state, the tax shall be computed on the aggregate income received from all districts and shall be certified for collection to the several taxing districts in proportion to the amount of income received from each under such rules and regulations as the tax commission may prescribe. *(1917 c. 246.)*

General laws as to personal property taxes applicable

SECTION 1087m—22. 4. All laws not in conflict with the provisions of this act, relating to the assessment, collection and payment of taxes on personal property, the correction of errors in assessment and tax rolls, the compromise or cancellation of illegal taxes and the refund of moneys paid thereon, shall be applicable to the income tax herein provided for; but no town or village board or common council, nor the county officers specified in section 1210g, shall compromise or cancel any income tax or any part thereof or refund any moneys paid thereon without the written approval of the assessor of incomes who made the assessment or of the tax commission in the case of assessments made by it, specifying the defect in the assessment or tax proceeding and the amount of taxable income which should have been assessed and the amount of the taxes justly chargeable thereto. *(1913 c. 27.)*

The foregoing section makes the statutory provisions relating to the manner of assessing, collecting and paying personal property taxes applicable to the income tax where no express provision to the contrary is made. It also permits the correction of errors in assessment and tax rolls by town, city and village clerks and treasurers in the manner and to the extent prescribed by sections 1065, 1085 and 1085a of the statutes.

Approval of a claim for illegal taxes by the assessor of incomes or the tax commission is not a condition precedent to an action in court to recover such taxes. *Field vs. Milwaukee,* 161 Wis.

393. But it is a condition precedent to voluntary payment or refund by town, village and county boards and common councils.

Delinquent income taxes

SECTION 1087m—22. 5. In the return of delinquent income taxes as required by law the entire amount of each such delinquent income tax shall be returned to the county treasurer without division or apportionment. All laws, including the provisions of any city charter in conflict with this subsection are hereby repealed. *(1913 c. 720.)*

How income taxes collected by wrong district recovered by proper district

(6) Whenever any city, town or village shall have collected an income tax that under the income tax law ought not to have been collected by such city, town or village, but by the provisions of the income tax law should have been collected by another town, city or village, such tax shall be paid to the town, city or village entitled thereto; provided, however, that no such payment shall be made except on the written approval of the assessor of incomes who made the assessment, or of the tax commission in the case of assessments made by it, specifying the defect in the assessment or tax proceeding; and provided further that a claim for such tax shall have been made within one year after the collection of the tax. If any portion of such taxes so refunded shall be properly chargeable to the county and state, they shall be so charged, and such town, city or village shall be credited by the county treasurer on the settlement with the proper treasurer for the taxes of the ensuing year, with the whole amount of such state and county taxes so paid into the county treasury; and the county treasurer shall also be allowed by the state treasurer the amount of said taxes so illegally collected and paid in his settlement with the state treasurer, next after the payment of such claim. *(1919 c. 306.)*

Apportionment of income tax

SECTION 1087m—23. All income taxes collected in cash over and above the personal property offset authorized by section 1087m—26 of the statutes shall be divided as follows, to wit: Ten per cent to the state, twenty per cent to the county, and the balance to the town, city or village in which the tax was assessed, levied and collected, except that when such balance exceeds two per cent of the equalized value of such town, city or village under section 1073, such excess shall be paid to the county to be distributed and paid to the several towns, cities and villages of the county, according to the school population therein.

The same shall be remitted and accounted for in the same manner as the state and county taxes collected from property are remitted and paid, except that income taxes returned delinquent shall not be charged to the county nor credited to the town, city or village returning the same. Out of the first moneys received and retained 'from cash collected from such income taxes in any city of the first class, however organized, there shall be transferred and paid to the firemen's pension fund provided for by chapter 165 of the laws of 1903 and laws amendatory thereof, a sum each year sufficient to make the said firemen's pensions fund on the first day of March in each year not less than one hundred and seventy-five thousand dollars, to be used for the purpose of paying pensions to disabled and superannuated members of the fire department and their beneficiaries mentioned in said laws. The county treasurer shall account for and pay all delinquent taxes thereafter collected by him, upon the basis hereinbefore provided, to the state treasurer, and to the several town, city and village treasurers entitled thereto quarterly thereafter. (1917 c. 485.)

This section is supplemented by section 19 of chapter 628, Laws of 1917, requiring county treasurers to pay to the state treasurer on or before the first day of May in each year the state's quota of all income taxes collected in cash as shown by the reports of local treasurers in their settlement with the county treasurers on the 22nd day of March preceding.

SECTION 1087m—24. 1. No commissioner, assessor of incomes, deputy, member of a county board of review, or any other officer, agent, clerk or employe shall divulge or make known to any person in any manner any information whatsoever obtained directly or indirectly by him in the discharge of his duties or permit any income return or copy thereof or any paper or book so obtained to be seen or examined by any person except as provided by law; provided, that any and all information contained in income tax returns and in the statements and correspondence pertaining thereto relating to the ownership or value of property shall be furnished or made accessible to all public officials charged with the duty of assessing the same for taxation or of supervising the assessment thereof, under such rules and regulations as the tax commission shall prescribe, but no information so received shall be divulged by any such official except as may be necessary in the proper performance of his duties; and provided further that in any action or proceeding brought for the collection, remission, cancellation or refund of the whole or any part of a tax assessed under sections 1087m—1 to 1087m—30, or for enforcing the penalties prescribed for making false or fraudulent returns, any and all information contained in such returns may be furnished or made accessible to the officers or representatives of the state or municipal district charged with the duty of prosecuting or defending the same, under such rules and regulations as the tax commission shall prescribe; and all such returns and the statements and correspondence relating thereto may be produced in evidence in any action or proceeding, civil or criminal, directly pertaining to such returns or the assessment made thereon. *(1919 c. 638.)*

The following rules and regulations have been prescribed by the tax commission to be observed in administering the foregoing section.

(1) The information contained in income tax returns which may be divulged is limited to such as relates to the "ownership and value of property," and may be furnished only to "public officials" charged with the duties of assessing the same for taxation.

The term "public officials" includes local assessors of property, income assessors, public administrators and boards of review.

(2) Any such public official is prohibited from divulging any information received by him except so far as "may be necessary for the performance of his duties."

(3) As income tax returns contain much information not relating to the ownership and value of property which cannot lawfully be disclosed, they should not be submitted to the inspection of assessing officials, and the disclosure authorized by the foregoing section must be confined strictly to information of the character specified therein.

(4) All the information contained in income tax returns relating to the ownership and value of property may be made available to "public officials charged with the duties of assessing the same for taxation" when called for during the assessing period and until the final adjournment of the board of review, and may be given orally or certified in writing as may be found most convenient or as may best serve the purpose of the public officials entitled thereto.

(5) Disclosure should not be made at any time except when assessing officers are engaged in the performance of their duties

and for no other purpose than to enable them to properly perform such duties.

(6) There should be furnished to the representatives of the state or municipality charged with the duty of prosecuting or defending any action or proceeding defined in the act a certified copy of the income tax return upon which the tax affected by such action or proceeding was based, and upon the hearing or trial thereof said return and all statements and correspondence relating thereto should be produced in evidence, if called for by the court or body before whom such action or proceeding is pending, or by the representatives of the state or municipality prosecuting or defending the same.

(7) Should an assessor of incomes be in doubt as to his duty to furnish the information called for in any case he should apply to the tax commission for further instructions.

Penalties on officials for violating secrecy of returns

2. Any officer, agent, clerk or employe violating any of the provisions of this section shall upon conviction thereof be punished by a fine of not less than one hundred dollars nor more than five hundred dollars, or by imprisonment in the county jail for not less than one month nor more than six months, or by imprisonment in the state prison for not more than two years, at the discretion of the court.

3. Such officer, agent, clerk or employe upon such conviction shall also forfeit his office or employment and shall be incapable of holding any public office in this state for a period of three years thereafter.

Tax commission authorized to make certain records public

4. Nothing herein shall be construed as preventing the assessment roll, the tax roll and all proceedings had before the county board of review and all evidence taken at such hearing from being open to public inspection at such times and under such conditions as the state tax commission may direct.

Under the authority of the above subdivision the commission entered the following order on the first day of October, 1913, and, except as modified by chapter 638, laws of 1919, the order is still in force.

To County Clerks:

Whereas, the proper officers of the several villages and cities of the state are required by law during the month of October of each year to estimate the amount of money necessary to defray the expenses of their respective municipalities for the ensuing year, and to levy a tax on the general property of such district for that purpose and in so doing are required to take into consideration the revenues available from all sources, including the amount to be derived under the income tax law, and,

Whereas, the income tax law provides that the assessment and tax rolls and all proceedings and evidence taken before the county board of review shall be open to public inspection, under such conditions as the tax commission may direct;

Now, Therefore, It is hereby ordered and directed that all assessment rolls, completed by the assessor and board of review and filed in your office, and all tax rolls as soon as convenient, be treated as public records, open to the inspection of persons having occasion to consult the same, to the same extent and in the same manner and under the same restrictions, as other public records in your custody. You are further directed not to make public or permit the examination of any return, exhibit, writing or proceeding in your possession or custody, relating to the assessment of income taxes, except the assessment and tax roll, hereinbefore referred to.

This rule is to be considered permanent until revoked or amended by the tax commission.

Personal property tax receipts may be offset against income tax—when

SECTION 1087m—26. Any person who shall have paid a tax assessed upon his personal property during any year shall be permitted to present the receipt therefor to the tax collector, together with any similar receipts for personal property taxes paid by members of his family whose incomes have been assessed to him, and have the same accepted by the tax collector to their full amount in the payment of income taxes assessed against such person during said year; provided, that no receipt for taxes paid on the shares of stock in any state, national or mutual savings bank or trust company shall be allowed as an offset against any income tax within the meaning of this section. If in any year a person failed or neglected, or shall in the future fail or neglect, to present his personal property tax receipt in payment of income tax as provided by this section, and the council of the city or board of the town or village to which such taxes shall have been paid is satisfied that such person was entitled to such offset, and that by reason thereof, such person has paid to the town, city or village an amount in excess of that which he was legally obliged to pay, it may within two years after such payment remit such excess to such person without interest and charge the state and county for their respective proportions of such excess, as provided in section 1164. *(1919. c. 143.)*

Upon payment of a tax assessed in 1913 for personal property omitted from the tax rolls in 1910 and 1911 through no fault of the taxpayer he is entitled under sec. 1087m—26 to have the amount so paid credited on his income tax assessed during 1913. *City of Milwaukee vs. Patton,* 158 Wis. 617.

Chapter 244, Laws of 1919, requires buildings on leased lands to be assessed as real estate.   Taxes paid thereon can not be used as offset against income taxes.

OFFSET OF INCOME TAX BY PERSONAL PROPERTY TAX

Directions to Wisconsin taxpayers

When the income tax and the personal property tax are both assessed in the same district and the taxpayer is not assessed for income tax in any other district, the taxpayer will simply pay the larger tax and obtain two receipts, one for personal property and one for income tax.

If the taxpayer wishes to use a personal tax receipt issued in one district to offset income tax assessed in another district, the following procedure should be observed:

1. Secure a separate personal property tax receipt and have the treasurer endorse on it the amount used to offset income tax in that district.

2. Present or mail this personal tax receipt to the Assessor of Incomes of the county in which it was issued and apply for Special Offset Receipts covering the balance of personal property tax.   In Milwaukee city apply first to Income Tax Teller, City Treasurer's Office.

3. This application should state the amount desired for offset in each other district in which the taxpayer has income tax to pay, giving the correct name of such district and the county in which situated.

4. Offset receipts for balance of personal property tax will be issued with coupons, which coupons will be accepted only for the amount entered upon them and in the district for which they are issued.

5. The taxpayer should pay his personal property taxes in time to secure special coupon receipts from the Assessor of Incomes and forward them to the local treasurer against whom they are issued. Penalties are imposed if the taxes are not paid on or before January 31.

6. Ordinary personal property tax receipts will not be received in offset in districts other than that in which issued.

7. The exact name is important. For instance, a firm cannot use its personal property tax receipt to offset the income tax of its members.

8. It is a common practice to write a personal property tax receipt at the bottom of the real estate receipt. Taxpayers should therefore request a separate personal tax receipt whenever they wish to use the latter to secure the special offset receipts mentioned above.

Assessment and collection of taxes for 1911 not affected by income tax law

SECTION 1087m—27. Nothing contained in this act shall be construed to affect the assessment or collection of taxes assessed in the year 1911 or prior thereto, under present laws, nor to limit the power of assessors and boards of review relative to correcting assessment rolls, placing omitted property thereon, and reassessing property whenever such correction, insertion of omitted property, or reassessment might be made under the laws as they now exist.

Tax commission may make rules and regulations

SECTION 1087m—28. The state tax commission is hereby empowered to make such rules and regulations as it shall deem necessary in order to carry out foregoing provisions.

Tax commission may employ clerks and specialists

SECTION 1087m—29. The state tax commission is hereby authorized to employ such clerks and specialists as are necessary to carry into effective operation this act. Salaries and compensations of such clerks and specialists shall be charged to the proper appropriation for the tax commission. *(1913 c. 772.)*

Local treasurer to be reimbursed for costs

SECTION 1087m—30. Whenever in any action for the recovery of an unlawful income tax, judgment is rendered against the city, town or village treasurer for such tax, the city, town or village shall reimburse such treasurer for such sums of money as may be recovered against him in any court, with the costs and expenses of suit, for any such income tax collected by him, and such city shall be reimbursed for the county's and state's share of such tax in the manner provided in section 1164 of the statutes. *(1915 c. 411.)*

By the voluntary payment of a tax all right to bring action to recover it back or question its legality is waived. *State ex rel. Marshall and Ilsley Bank,* 155 Wis. 499. Proceedings to recover an illegal tax must be commenced within one year after payment. See sec. 1164 **R**. S.

RECEIPTS TAXABLE AS INCOME AND EXPENDITURES NOT ALLOWABLE AS DEDUCTIONS

The forms of returns prescribed for taxpayers and the law defining income are so detailed and definite as to leave little room for misunderstanding and no excuse for omitting items of taxable income. In brief, all gains or profits received during the year should be reported as income, and all ordinary expenses incurred in producing such income are allowable as deductions.

Nevertheless in the administration of the law numerous questions have arisen as to whether a given receipt should be treated as income or a particular expenditure allowed as a deduction. Without attempting to cover the entire ground we enumerate below the most common of these items, specifying in two separate groups certain receipts which should be treated as income and certain expenditures which are not allowable as deductions. It should be borne in mind that these lists do not purport to be exhaustive nor to include all items of income or deduction, but are confined to those which have occasioned most controversy.

RECEIPTS TAXABLE AS INCOME

1. All compensation for personal or professional services, whether in the form of wages, salaries, fees or commissions.

2. Salaries and wages of all state and local officers, including judges.

3. All salaries, stipends and gifts received by clergymen in their own right in the performance of their pastoral duties.

4. The reasonable value of accommodations furnished to officers and employes as part of their salary, such as board and lodging to hotel managers, and use of residences furnished to pastors, teachers and public employes.

5. All rent of Wisconsin real estate, including royalties received for extracting ore.

6. All interest on bonds and mortgages whether executed by parties or secured by property within or without the state.

7. All dividends declared out of profits accumulated since the 1st of January, 1911, which have not been taxed to the corporation distributing the same.

8. Stock dividends to the same extent and under the same circumstances as cash dividends.

9. All profits derived from property located or business transacted within the state.

10. All profits from the sale of Wisconsin real estate or other capital assets accrued since the first day of January, 1911.

11. The reasonable value of farm products consumed by the owner and of all supplies from a merchant's stock used by his family.

12. Income from inheritances, bequests and trust estates.

13. Dividends from state and national banks not taxed under Wisconsin laws.

14. Dividends declared by corporations from depreciation reserve.

15. Endowment or other life insurance paid to the insured in his lifetime in excess of the premiums paid therefor.

16. Dividends declared from reserve fund to cover depreciation or bad accounts.

EXPENDITURES NOT ALLOWABLE AS DEDUCTIONS

1. Alimony to divorced wife.

2. Depreciation of land or of property not producing taxable income.

3. Depreciation of good will or from obsolescence.

4. Depletion of mines claimed by lessee.

5. Election expenses.

6. Administrators', executors' and attorneys' fees in probating estates.

7. Interest paid by a corporation in the operation of a business or the maintenance of property not producing taxable income.

8. Losses sustained in the transaction of business the income of which, if any, would not be taxable.

9. Uncollectable rent and interest not previously reported as income.

10. Premiums paid by corporations and partnerships for insurance on the lives of corporate officers or members.

11. Expenses incurred in the organization of a corporation.

12. Special assessments for street, sewer and sidewalk improvements.

13. Taxes on property from which no taxable income is derived.

14. Wages of household servants, chauffeurs or nurses.

15. Shrinkage or depreciation in the market value of stocks, bonds or other securities until sold or otherwise finally disposed of.

DEPRECIATION PERCENTAGES

After a careful examination of the question of the amount of depreciation sustained by property of various kinds the tax commission has arrived at the following percentages as representing the average annual rate of "depreciation by use, wear and tear of property from which the income is derived," assuming that it is kept in a fair state of repair. These rates only will be allowed as a maximum unless unusual and extraordinary circumstances can be conclusively proved to warrant a greater allowance. They should be applied to the original cost value of the property in computing the amount of the depreciation claim. No claim for depreciation on account of obsolescence can be allowed under the Wisconsin law.

ANNUAL DEPRECIATION IN PERCENTAGES

Buildings	Frame and veneered, per cent	Brick and masonry, per cent	Fireproof, per cent
Sheds	7		
Stables, etc.	4	3	
Farm dwellings	1.5	1.5	
Other farm dwellings	2.5	1.5	
City dwellings	2.5	1.5	1
Apartment houses	.3	2.5	1.25
Stores	2.5	2	
Stores with flats above	2.5	2	
Warehouses	2.5	2	1.25
Elevators	2.5	1.75	1.25
Factories	5	3	1.25
Office buildings	2.5	1.5	1
Hotels	2.5	1.75	1.5
Paper and pulp mills		2.5	2

MACHINERY, DIES, PATTERNS, SMALL TOOLS AND DRAWINGS

Machinery ....3 to 10 per cent
Dies ....20 per cent
Patterns ....25 per cent
Small Tools ....25 per cent
Drawings ....30 per cent

MISCELLANEOUS PROPERTY

Horses ....16 per cent
Harness ....20 per cent
Wagons ....16 per cent
Sleighs ....10 per cent
Automobiles ....20 to 25 per cent

OTHER PROPERTY

Depreciation of other property not listed above should be computed upon the cost value and for the actual exhaustion during the year sustained from use, wear and tear.

CHAPTER 667, LAWS OF 1919

SOLDIERS BONUS ACT

SECTION 1. The service recognition board is hereby created to consist of the governor, the adjutant general and *a returned soldier to be appointed by the governor.*

SECTION 2. For the purpose of raising a sum sufficient to assure to each soldier, sailor, marine and nurse, including Red Cross nurses, who served in the armed forces of the United

States during the war against Germany and Austria, and who at the time of his or her induction into the service was a resident of Wisconsin, a sum not exceeding ten dollars for each month of service, with a minimum of fifty dollars, as a token of appreciation of the character and spirit of their patriotic service, and to perpetuate such appreciation as a part of the history of Wisconsin, a tax of not exceeding three mills on each dollar of the assessed valuation in addition to the income surtax hereinafter mentioned is hereby levied and authorized to be included in the next tax levy; provided that in case any county shall elect by resolution of the county board of such county, adopted prior to the levy of such tax, to raise said amount by a bond issue, authority is hereby conferred upon said county to issue such bond and thereupon the proper authorities shall remit said levy in such county. If any such person entitled to the benefits under this act be deceased before receiving such payment, then the payment accruing to said deceased shall be paid to the surviving widow, child or children, mother or dependent father, in the order herein stated, and in such case July 1, 1919, shall be deemed the date of termination of such service. The benefit of this act shall not accrue to any person for time spent while taking training in any student army training camp, nor to any person who, though inducted into service, did civilian work at civilian pay.

SECTION 3. All sums levied and collected by taxation or raised by the issue of bonds by any county shall be paid into the state treasury and held there as a special fund to be known as the service recognition fund and disbursed upon certificates of the service recognition board, as to the persons entitled thereto and the amount to which each person is entitled.

SECTION 4. The service recognition board shall have complete charge and control of the general scheme of such payments. It shall adopt general rules, uniform throughout the state, for the distribution of said fund, the ascertainment and selection of proper beneficiaries and the amounts to which beneficiaries are entitled, and for procedure, and may select or create such agents as it may deem necessary.

SECTION 5. Subsection (5) of section 658 of the Statutes is renumbered to be subsection (6) thereof.

SECTION 6. There is added to section 658 of the Statutes a new subsection to read: (Section 658) (5) For the purpose of carrying out the provisions of chapter 452 of the laws of 1919; but bonds issued in any county for such purpose shall not exceed in amount three mills on each dollar of the total assessed valuation of such county.

SECTION 7. (1) In addition to the normal tax imposed by section 1087m—6 of the statutes, there shall be levied, collected and paid upon the incomes of all persons, except as otherwise provided by law, a surtax on taxable income computed at the following rates, to wit:

(a) On the fourth one thousand dollars or any part thereof, one and three-fourths per cent;

(b) On the fifth one thousand dollars or any part thereof, two per cent;

(c) On the sixth one thousand dollars or any part thereof, two and one-half per cent;

(d) On the seventh one thousand dollars or any part thereof, three per cent;

(e) On the eighth one thousand dollars or any part thereof, three and one-half per cent;

(f) On the ninth one thousand dollars or any part thereof, four per cent;

(g) On the tenth one thousand dollars or any part thereof, four and one-half per cent;

(h) On the eleventh one thousand dollars or any part thereof, five per cent;

(i) On the twelfth one thousand dollars or any part thereof, five and one-half per cent;

(j) On any sum taxable as income in excess of twelve thousand dollars, six per cent.

(2) In addition to the normal tax imposed by section 1087m—6 of the statutes, there shall be levied, collected and paid upon the incomes of corporations, joint stock companies or associations, except as otherwise provided by law, a surtax on taxable income computed at the following rates, to wit:

On the first one thousand dollars or any part thereof, two per cent;

On the second one thousand dollars or any part thereof, two and one-half per cent;

On the third one thousand dollars or any part thereof, three per cent;

On the fourth one thousand dollars or any part thereof, three and one-half per cent;

On the fifth one thousand dollars or any part thereof, four per cent;

On the sixth one thousand dollars or any part thereof, five per cent;

On the seventh one thousand dollars or any part thereof, six per cent;

On all taxable income in excess of seven thousand dollars, six per cent.

(3) In computing the tax upon income of corporations, joint stock companies or associations, there shall be deducted before such tax is computed from the net income an amount equal to six per cent of its capital stock, surplus and undivided profits.

(4) The surtax provided for herein shall be upon the income received during the year ending December 31, 1918, and shall be returned, assessed and collected in the same manner and at the same time as is provided for the return, assessment and payment of the normal income tax provided for under sections 1087m—1 to 1087m—30, both inclusive, except as otherwise herein provided.

(5) Deductions and exemptions as are provided by law in the assessment of the normal income tax under section 1087m—6 shall be the same with respect to the assessment of this surtax, but said deductions and exemptions shall not be additional thereto and shall only be made once.

(6) In the collection of said surtax the tax collector shall give his separate receipt therefor and there shall be no offset upon the personal property tax, and section 1087m—26 shall not apply to said surtax.

(7) The whole amount collected as surtax shall, through the same channels as other income taxes are paid, be paid into the state treasury, and section 1087m—23 of the statutes shall not apply to said surtax. The amount so paid into the state treasury shall be set apart for the service recognition fund.

(8) The service recognition board shall estimate or cause to be estimated the amount which may be collected under this section and determine as nearly as practicable the balance needed for said fund, which balance shall be raised by taxation or bond issues as provided by section 2 of this act.

SECTION 8. There is appropriated from the service recognition fund in the state treasury to the service recognition board:

(1) Such sums as may be necessary to pay each soldier, sailor, marine and nurse, including Red Cross nurses, who served in the armed forces of the United States during the war against Germany and Austria, and who at the time of his or her induction into the service was a resident of Wisconsin, a sum not exceeding ten dollars for each month of service, with a minimum of fifty dollars.

(2) Such sums as may be necessary to cover the cost of administering this act.

SECTION 9. A special election shall be held on Tuesday, September 2, 1919, at which the following question shall be submitted: "Shall there be levied in the year 1919, a mill tax of not to exceed three mills on the dollar and an income tax sufficient to raise an aggregate sum of approximately fifteen million dollars to be paid by the state to Wisconsin, soldiers, sailors, marines and nurses as stated in chapter 667 of the laws of 1919?"

SECTION 10. Such special election shall be conducted, held and noticed and the ballots to be used thereat shall be prepared, printed and distributed and the ballots cast thereat shall be counted, canvassed and returned in the same manner as is by law provided in the case of the submission of a proposed constitutional amendment to a vote of the people. The state board of canvassers shall not meet to canvass such election returns. The secretary of state shall within ten days after the receipt of the returns from the different county clerks canvass, certify, record and publish as in the case of a constitutional amendment the number of ballots cast in favor of such proposed recognition and the number of ballots cast against such proposed recognition.

SECTION 11. If a majority of the votes cast at such special election are in favor of the recognition of Wisconsin soldiers, sailors, marines and nurses as provided upon such ballots, then the necessary taxes shall be levied in the year 1919.

The foregoing act was ratified by the people at a special election held on September 2, 1919. The surtax imposed by it will appear on the tax-rolls of 1919 and will be payable to the local treasurers at the same time other taxes are payable. The surtax must be paid wholly in cash.

Educational bonus act

At the special session of the legislature in September, 1919, an act was passed, imposing a second or additional surtax on incomes received in 1918 and on incomes received annually thereafter for a term of four years. That part of the act providing for the additional surtax reads as follows:

SECTION 5. (1) In addition to the normal tax imposed by section 1087m—6 of the statutes, and the surtax imposed by chapter 667 of the laws of 1919, there shall be levied, collected and paid upon the incomes of all persons, annually for five years, except as otherwise provided by law, a surtax on taxable income computed at the following rates to wit:

(a) On the fourth one thousand dollars or any part thereof, seven twentieths of one per cent;

(b) On the fifth one thousand dollars or any part thereof, four-tenths of one per cent;

(c) On the sixth one thousand dollars or any part thereof, five-tenths of one per cent;

(d) On the seventh one thousand dollars or any part thereof, six-tenths of one per cent;

(e) On the eighth one thousand dollars or any part thereof, seven-tenths of one per cent;

(f) On the ninth one thousand dollars or any part thereof, eight-tenths of one per cent;

(g) On the tenth one thousand dollars or any part thereof, nine-tenths of one per cent;

(h) On the eleventh one thousand dollars or any part thereof, one per cent;

(i) On the twelfth one thousand dollars or any part thereof, one and one-tenth per cent;

(j) On any sum taxable income in excess of twelve thousand dollars, one and two-tenths per cent.

(2) In addition to the normal tax imposed by section 1087m—6 of the statutes, and the surtax imposed by chapter 667, laws of 1919, there shall be levied, collected and paid upon the incomes of corporations, joint stock companies or associations, except as otherwise provided by law, annually for five years, a surtax on taxable income computed at the following rates, to wit:

On the first one thousand dollars or any part thereof, four-tenths of one per cent;

On the second one thousand dollars or any part thereof, five-tenths of one per cent;

On the third one thousand dollars or any part thereof, six-tenths of one per cent;

On the fourth one thousand dollars or any part thereof, seven-tenths of one per cent;

On the fifth one thousand dollars or any part thereof, eight-tenths of one per cent;

On the sixth one thousand dollars or any part thereof, one per cent;

On the seventh one thousand dollars or any part thereof, one and two tenths per cent;

On all taxable income in excess of seven thousand dollars, one and two-tenths per cent.

(3) In computing the tax upon income of corporations, joint stock companies or associations, there shall be deducted before such tax is computed from the net income an amount equal to six per cent of its capital stock, surplus and undivided profits at the beginning of the taxable year.

(4) The first surtax provided for herein shall be upon the income received during the year ending December 31, 1918, or corresponding fiscal year for which the taxpayer reported his income under the general income tax law and annually thereafter for four years, and shall be returned, assessed and collected in the same manner and at the same time as is provided for the return, assessment and payment of the normal income tax provided for under sections 1087m—1 to 1087m—30, both inclusive, except as otherwise herein provided.

(5) Deductions and exemptions as are provided by law in the assessment of the normal income tax under section 1087m—6 shall be the same with respect to the assessment of this surtax,

but said deductions and exemptions shall not be additional thereto and shall only be made once.

(6) In the collection of said surtax the tax collector shall give his receipt therefor and there shall be no offset upon the personal property tax, and section 1087m—26 shall not apply to said surtax.

(7) The whole amount collected as surtax shall, through the same channels as other income taxes are paid, be paid into the state treasury, and section 1087m—23 of the statutes shall not apply to said surtax. The amount so paid into the state treasury shall be available for the purposes of this act.

The first or ''soldiers' bonus'' surtax, in case of individuals, is found by deducting from the normal income tax $37.50, representing the amount of the normal tax on the first $3,000 of income which is not subject to the tax. The surtax on an income in excess of $3,000 is computed at the same rates as the normal tax.

The second or additional surtax is one-fifth of the soldiers' bonus surtax.

Surtaxes cannot be paid with personal property tax receipts but must be paid in cash.

PART III

DUTIES OF ASSESSORS OF INCOMES IN CONNECTION WITH GENERAL PROPERTY TAXATION

SECTION 1087b. (1) The assessor of incomes shall have full and complete supervision and direction of the work of the town, city and village assessors of the county or counties within his assessment district and shall annually, on or before the last Tuesday of April, call a meeting for each such county of all such local assessors for conference and instruction relative to their duties in the valuation and assessment of all property subject to taxation. Each such local assessor, upon notice by mail from said assessor of incomes shall attend such meeting, and shall receive therefor the sum of three dollars, and also six cents per mile for travel from his residence to the county seat and returning. Such compensation shall be paid out of the treasury of the county in which such local assessor resides upon the certificate of the assessor of incomes showing such attendance and travel, in like manner as certificates of witnesses and jurors are paid.

(2) The assessor of incomes shall have access to all public records, books, papers and offices throughout his district and shall make a full and complete examination of them and investigate all other matters and subjects relative to the assessment and taxation of property in the several towns, villages and cities contained therein; and for that purpose he shall visit each such town, village and city as often as may be necessary during each year.

(3) The assessor of incomes shall examine and test the work of assessors during the progress of their assessments and ascertain whether any of them is assessing property at other than full value or is omitting property subject to taxation from the roll. He shall have the rights and powers of a local assessor for the examination of persons and property and for the discovery of property subject to taxation, and shall have the power to personally value and reassess any property previously assessed by the local assessor. If he shall ascertain that any property has been omitted or not assessed according to law, he shall bring the same to the attention of the local assessor of the proper district and if such local assessor shall neglect or refuse to correct the assessment he shall report the fact in writing to the clerk of the proper board of review at or before the meeting of such board

and such clerk shall lay the same before said board of review for its action.

(4) Whenever the assessor of incomes ascertains, or has good reason to believe, that any assessor is guilty of a violation of law, he is authorized to make complaint to the presiding judge of the circuit court for the removal of such assessor. The district attorney shall attend and prosecute such proceedings for removal.

(5) The assessor of incomes shall make a report to the county board of each county within his assessment district showing in detail the work of local assessors in their several districts, the failure, if any, of such assessors or property owners to comply with the law, the relative assessed and true value of property in each local assessment district, and all such information and statistics as he may obtain which will be of assistance to the county board in determining the relative value of all taxable property in each town, city and village in the county. Such report shall be filed with the county clerk at least fifteen days before the annual meeting of the county board. The county clerk shall cause to be printed not less than two hundred copies of such report, one of which shall be mailed immediately by the county clerk to each member of the county board. Not less than six copies of such printed report, together with all statistics accompanying the same, shall be filed with the state tax commission.

(6) The county board, upon its own motion, may direct the assessor of incomes to make a reassessment of all the taxable property in any local assessment district for any year, and to report the same in the form of an assessment roll to the county board at its next annual session. In making such reassessment, the value of the property shall be fixed, as nearly as may be, as of the time the original assessment was made, and he shall have the powers and be governed by the rules provided by law for local assessors in the assessment of property for taxation. In case the aggregate valuation of taxable property as determined by such reassessment, shall be ten per cent or more in excess of the aggregate valuation thereof as fixed by the original assessment, the expense of making such reassessment, not exceeding five dollars per day for each day necessarily and actually spent in making the same, shall be charged to such local assessment district in the next apportionment thereto of county taxes.

(7) The state tax commission shall call a meeting of the assessors of incomes at the capitol at a specified time in the month of January in each year, for a conference on the subjects of taxation and the administration of the laws, and for the instruction of such officers in their duties. The actual and necessary expenses of each such officer in such attendance shall be audited and paid out of the state treasury in the same manner as other expenses of said assessors are audited and paid. *(1913 c. 443.)*

This section gives assessors of incomes "complete supervision and direction" of the work of local assessors within their respective districts and authorizes them to "value and reassess property." For this purpose every assessor of incomes is authorized to inspect all statements, records, and memoranda in any public office in his district relating to the assessment and value of property therein, and to examine persons and property to the same extent and with the same authority as local assessors.

It should be borne in mind, however, that the powers conferred upon assessors of incomes are advisory only. Their authority to appraise property and examine taxpayers is only for the purpose of testing the work of the regular assessors and presenting the result of such investigation to the proper board of review or county board. They are not authorized to change the local assessor's valuations nor to insert their own valuations on the assessment roll. Even the reassessments required to be made by direction of the county board under subdivision 6 of this section are not reassessments in the proper sense and can only be used as an aid to the county board in making the county equalization. There is no authority in this statute for inserting such reassessment values in the assessment roll nor substituting them for the valuation of the local assessor.

INDEX

CPSIA information can be obtained
at www.ICGtesting.com
Printed in the USA
BVHW04*1059010818
523278BV00012B/188/P